Confession and complicity
in narrative

Confession and complicity in narrative

DENNIS A. FOSTER

Department of English,
Southern Methodist University

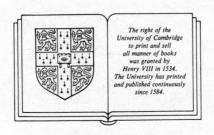

The right of the
University of Cambridge
to print and sell
all manner of books
was granted by
Henry VIII in 1534.
The University has printed
and published continuously
since 1584.

CAMBRIDGE UNIVERSITY PRESS

Cambridge
London   New York   New Rochelle
Melbourne   Sydney

Published by the Press Syndicate of the University of Cambridge
The Pitt Building, Trumpington Street, Cambridge CB2 1RP
32 East 57th Street, New York, NY 10022, USA
10 Stamford Road, Oakleigh, Melbourne 3166, Australia

First published 1987

Printed in Great Britain at
the University Press, Cambridge

British Library cataloguing in publication data
Foster, Dennis A.
Confession and complicity in narrative.
1. Desire in literature
I. Title
809'.93353   PN56.D/

Library of Congress cataloguing in publication data
Foster, Dennis A.
Confession and complicity in narrative.
1. Reader-response criticism.   2. Confession stories –
History and criticism.   I. Title.
PN98.R38F67   1987   801'.95   86-33404

ISBN 0 521 34191 4

To Nina

Contents

Abbreviations

The following abbreviations will be used for page references for the major texts:

AA   *Absalom, Absalom!*
C   Augustine's *Confessions*
Diary   *Diary of a Seducer*
FC   'The Figure in the Carpet'
SW   *The Kiss of the Spider Woman*
SL   *The Scarlet Letter*
UN   *The Unnamable*

Acknowledgements

I do not know if most books are as indebted to the generosity of readers as this one is. From the largest conceptions to the most minute matters of style, readers have told me what they liked and what they did not. My earliest readers were also those from whom I probably stole most freely: Philip Kuberski, Robert Gregory, and Nina Schwartz. The processes of reading and revision have made it difficult in places for me to tell my own work from theirs. That experience has been the most optimistic confirmation of the thesis of this book. I must also thank my former teachers, Alexander Gelley and John Carlos Rowe, who in their early readings of my manuscript chose encouragement over caution in their advice. And the careful reading John Paul Riquelme gave an intermediate version of the text contributed greatly to what economy the book now displays.

During the long process of revision, I often doubted the patience of Cambridge University Press. The occasional but dependable good-humored encouragement of Andrew Brown and Terence Moore's practical advice were valuable supports. It is hard to acknowledge the anonymous readers the Press found to read and evaluate versions of this book. They were a source of advice I had not expected, but their comments were instrumental to the ultimate shape this book took.

Earlier versions of two chapters of this book, on *The Scarlet Letter* and on *The Unnamable*, have appeared in *Criticism* and *Boundary 2*, respectively.

1

The confessional turn

The function of language is not to inform but to evoke. What I seek in speech is the response of the other. What constitutes me as subject is my question.

Lacan, *Écrits*

This is an essay about the motives for narrative. It arose from the problems attending the attempts of formalist theories to establish the boundaries of literary works and to exclude the wills and desires of writers and readers in the process of literary production. The idea that a poem, story, or novel could be understood as discrete, closed to the intrusion of other texts and authors, has provided limits to interpretation, assurances of meaning that console both readers and writers in the face of the endless interpretability of the open world. Recently, semiotic and post-structural literary theories have forced an acknowledgement of what we have always known, but perhaps not wanted to know: all writing exists in a larger world of writing, of intertextuality. The implications of such a context for the reading of literature are exciting to some – a promise of interpretive freedom – but discouraging to others, since interpretations of particular works can never be more than provisional, always contingent upon a wider horizon of writing. The meaning of a work cannot be found within its own boundaries.

At its most profound level, this notion of intertextuality unsettles the relation of writers to their productions. Despite the separation of writer from work in New Critical theory, the author remains the ultimate unifier of the text because the text represents an ultimately unified authorial consciousness. Helpful as it may be for readers to be assured of finding a meaning in the poem they are reading, can it compare with the writer's comfort in knowing that he or she is the source, if not the embodiment itself, of that meaning? New Criticism has maintained its lingering influence largely due to the anxiety that writers feel at the thought of giving up that status, and that readers would feel if that fountainhead were lost. Yet this loss of the author

1

and authority is at the heart of contemporary theory, for it is not just the work that is opened to the universe of textuality; it is also the writers. The language they write with is not their own, their parents are not theirs to choose, and the meanings of the words they put down are not theirs to decide. From the past that intrudes into every aspect of language to a 'posterity' continuously appropriating every production to its own desires, the personal, authentic genius of each writer is dispersed along a thousand paths. All that should be original is given over to repetition; every story is an interpretation of those that have preceded it. And yet writers continue to produce narratives.

Their motives are not likely to be conscious, but when an attempt is made to speak them, the attempts appear more as symptoms of desires at work in writing than as accurate representations of what occurs. They tend to reflect various articulations of a communication model of language, models of expression, revelation, representation that assume the existence of a reality to be communicated to another. They imply the linguistic externalization of a personal knowledge, a knowledge peculiar to the writer as a perception, a feeling, a recognition. The work manifests what is the writer's own, peculiar originality. This conception of the writer's relation to the work reflects the hope that the work will equal the self, a hope founded in the unity of the sign where meanings truly were on the other side of the signifying coin. Consequently, the very discourse of representation as expression is symptomatic of the desire for a language that will make the writer the master of his meanings.

Confession may provide a form for exploring the motives for narrative. It seems clearly to be based on a model of communication, and yet it has been exploited by writers because it provides room for evasion. Usually, it involves a narrator disclosing a secret knowledge to another, as a speaker to a listener, writer to reader, confessor to confessor. A full confession would presumably require that a private knowledge be revealed in a way that would allow another to understand, judge, forgive, and perhaps even sympathize. In most confessions, of course, the forms of expression are purely conventional, an acknowledgement of the predictable, almost ritualistic nature of most sin. A confessor speaks in guilt, feeling estranged from God and, consequently, strange to himself. The ordinary failings of human nature are universal and all the sinner's words need to do is acknowledge that nature, not specify the sin. A listener would presume he already knew the essential story, as if the language were transparent rather than conventional. Consequently, to be absolved, it is enough to submit to the rite of the sacrament.

The great sinner, one who has strayed so far that he requires a book to hold his confession, would seem to be another matter, would seem to need more than convention to reveal his supposedly extraordinary sin. His words suffer the same limitation as other men's, but with this difference: where the usual confession arouses little interest, the writer's narrative says the truth is hard to tell and you must work to understand. I could not simplify the sin of Adam – nor Augustine, nor Dimmesdale – to the cliché of saying they loved women too much, though a woman is central to each story. For at the moment the supposedly sinful act occurs, faith has already lapsed. Still confessors speak of wine and women, hatred, and greed as if they were the cause of conscience's pain, while the mysterious loss suffered in sinning remains unrelieved. At best, the sufferer can articulate this sense of loss and thereby enjoy the small comfort of recognizing himself as lost. But then what has he told his listener? The listener is also only human, also a sinner. Putting a priest's formal powers of absolution aside, he is no different from the speaker. How could he not be infected with the doubt and loss evoked by the narrative of confession? He traffics in the sins of others, which must at some level recall to him his own sins, his own estrangement from God's coherent being.

The confessional narrative occurs, then, between two substantial, unsettled subjects. By 'subject' I do not mean an autonomous, centered being that founds the individual, but the representation of the self, particularly as it is objectified through language. The subject is that aspect of the self available to understanding. For those whose language is completely normative, the subject will be stable, though hardly individual. But the speakers in the texts I am examining have violated the norms of their language and defied conventional authority, making them comprehensible only as the extravagancies of sin or greatness – that is, they become outlaws, strange no matter how often seen. They may describe deeds of lust and betrayal or, like Socrates, recount searches for the perfect good, but neither sin nor truth are presented in their narratives. By calling on the listeners' need to understand, what they can do is evoke in them a sense of loss that is experienced as a desire for truth: that is, they can unsettle the listeners' sense of self-possession.

3

This effect depends on a shared expectation of understanding implicit in the confessional relation, an expectation which, in the case of the writer's confession, is not discarded, but deferred as the conclusion fails to arrive: the writer will keep trying to tell the story if the reader will keep trying to understand. There is a conflict here between intention (to reveal the truth) and effect. Intention is not the origin of truth; as Nietzsche declared well before Wimsatt or even Freud, 'intention is merely a sign and symptom that still requires interpretation' (44). Specifically, it is a symptom of the narrator's desire to master his story. The issue is not persuasion, for there is no urging of a position; it is seduction. Obliged to understand, the listener abandons his position as one who knows and consents to listen, and thereby he enters the evasive discourse of the narrator, tracing a path that inevitably misses the encounter with truth.

We have lost the Author, the master of meanings, intentions, and language. But we have something more interesting, even if more insidious: a master who doesn't know, a leader with no course. The writer in this view has no truth, but has a language that has developed out of the labor and accidents of life, something peculiar to him, his to use but not fully to control: a discourse. This essay argues that the writer and reader meet in a discourse, less in a generous desire to share than in contention: the writer attempting to perpetuate his discourse, the reader attempting to appropriate it to his own uses. The result is the life of a work in an ever-expanding field of texuality as readers become writers interpreting, imitating, and denying what they read.

'The story was compelling,' we tend to say, even when we disclaim a conventional interest in character, plot, and closure. We like to be drawn by a story toward some conclusive interpretation. For most practiced readers, not even the most surprising, incongruous event has the freedom of pure contingency: the promise of organicism survives as a source of coherence and meaning. Hegel points to the attraction of the model to reasonable thought: 'The necessity in what takes place is hidden, and shows itself only in the End, but in such a way that this very End shows that necessity has also been there from the beginning' (Hegel 157). Within an organic model of reading, something can seem to stray beyond the boundaries only because its necessity has not yet been revealed through the illumination of the

End, the promise of which makes the events' apparent straying all the more intriguing.

For Hegel, however, this notion of interpretation would be justified in only the most banal of texts, if at all. It is based on the narcissistic delusion of total mastery, on the idea that Reason can fully understand. Reason begins by looking to find itself reflected in the reasonable things of the observable world. The ultimate consequence of this assumption is that it 'no longer aims to *find* itself *immediately*, but to produce itself by its own activity. It is *itself* the End at which its action aims.' Organicism, that is, sustains the readers' belief that their own reasonableness can be found everywhere. And if Reason suspects that what it finds in the world is merely the arbitrary imposition of its own features, it obscures the 'disgracefulness of the irrational, crude thought . . . by unthinkingly mixing up with it all sorts of relationships of cause and effect, or "sign," "organ," etc.' (Hegel 209). The lofty activities of reasonable thought are a search for self under the guise of an objective examination of the world, interpretation here being a screen to rationalize vanity.

A confession is both a challenge and a temptation to a rational reader. Reason in the sense I have presented it is more than a mode of thought: it is a faith in the explicability of the world and, more importantly, in the existence and coherence of the thinking self. The confessor is a species of madman, someone whose deviance into sin suggests the fragility, possibly the illusion, of reason's grasp on knowledge. The desire to understand such tales is motivated in part by the pleasure of mastery, but linked to that pleasure is an obligation: you cannot count on knowing yourself if you cannot make sense of this other. Like the story told by the ancient mariner, it sets the listener to work.

The connection between the narratives of the confessor and the madman is strengthened by the sense of anxious obligation that often appears in Freud's texts. The challenge presented by his patients' stories was different from that which deviant disciples such as Jung offered to his mastery.[1] His neurotics challenged the idea of reason itself. In the case history of the Wolfman, for example, Freud repeatedly returns to the elusive episodes of the Wolfman's childhood, events confessed (or created), Freud says, only under the pressure of Freud's threatened withdrawal. But having elicited the tale, he cannot make sense of it and cannot, as history has shown, release his patient from his neurosis. The obligation to understand, however, does not let Freud go, and he introduces a series of explanatory structures to fulfill his debt: chronologies, patterns of displacement, of cause and effect, metaphorics. These explanations sit uneasily beside (and beneath, in footnotes) each other, and are made more uneasy by the subsequent additions Freud made to the text over the years.

The Wolfman's case – like Schreber's, like Dora's – unsettled Freud. He must also have been disturbed by the Wolfman's amusement with analysis and the interest he showed in setting Freud to work on his case, an amusement Freud attributes to repression. Each case presents personal and theoretical challenges to Freud's practice by recalling both his own personal inadequacy as a doctor and suggesting the ultimate inadequacy of his psychoanalysis either to understand or to cure. There is something in Freud's narratives that resembles the guilt and obligation that motivate the confessing sinner. And like the sinner, Freud would rather admit to a personal failing than allow the possibility that the sustaining order of his universe might be a delusion.

Freud does not hesitate in his later texts to report his own failures, as if he had learned something from the Wolfman's amusement, something about revenge. At the end of the still disturbing *Beyond the Pleasure Principle*, he points to 'the starting point for fresh investigations' that 'in turn raises a host of other questions': 'We must be patient and await fresh methods and occasions of research. We must be ready, too, to abandon a path that we have followed for a time, if it seems to be leading to no good end' (Freud, *Beyond* 57–8). Far from being an admission of failure, this plea for patience complements a theoretical claim made early in the text that the ego, under the influence of the 'reality principle,' 'does not abandon the intention of ultimately obtaining pleasure, but it nevertheless demands and carries into effect the postponement of satisfaction, the abandonment of a number of possibilities of gaining satisfaction and the temporary toleration of unpleasure as a step on the long indirect road to pleasure' (Freud, *Beyond* 4). In repeating the metaphor of the detour (applied first to his patients' histories, then to his own writing), Freud suggests the secret satisfactions he obtains in failing to conclude his text: in leaving the tale unfinished, his readers would be obliged to work through what he had only begun. If he has been tormented by the stories he hears, many more people are fated to share his condition when they pick up his books.

The confessional relation, as I am presenting it, is not limited to religion or fiction. The works by Hegel and Freud that I mention suggest, rather, that narratives of many kinds reproduce patterns of power, desire, guilt and obligation that I find in confession.[2] When the knowledge offered by a text cannot be formulated within the rigid coding of a positive science, narrative is enlisted, a story whose message should be implicit, even though it may not be clear. Much, perhaps the most important knowledge of every culture, is contained and trans.nitted by the narratives that each of us is told, reproducing us in the image of our world.[3] And when I claim that much narrative is informed by desire and obligation, I am also claiming that this narrative is allied with the grounds of passion provided by the family and religion, and with the stories they tell. Confession is not an incidental narrative form within these institutions: it is a mode by which people enter into the discourse of their culture, where they step beyond reiteration of the stories and into interpretation. It represents an attempt to understand the terms and the limits by which the people are defined, both as they listen to the confessions of others and as they recount their own transgressions. It is this demand for understanding that other narratives will repeat as an integral part of their production and effect.

The ultimate failure of even the most didactic narratives to deliver a clear, direct knowledge suggests a fundamental discontinuity between understanding (as a kind of mastery) and the knowledge being transmitted. And yet the failure to understand can mean one risks sin and pain. It is as if what narrative teaches is ignorance, every reader's lack of knowledge; it is a lesson that ensures the struggle to understand will find no conclusion. I am suggesting that this lesson of ignorance with its burden of passion is carried over to subsequent narratives. It helps explain why the story is so compelling.

There is something primordial about the motivations I am suggesting, something learned before understanding for its own sake could have been an interest. That is, the desire to understand – and the guilt and fear experienced in finding that one does not understand – repeats an earlier experience. Psychoanalysis provides one explanation for this repetition. Freud suggests that the drive we feel toward understanding is modeled on a drive much more primary.

Writing of the fabulous achievements of modern man, Freud notes the dominance of the past in all movements into the future:

> What appears in a minority of human individuals as an untiring impulsion towards further perfection can easily be understood as a result of the instinctual repression upon which is based all that is most precious in human civilization. The repressed instinct never ceases to strive for complete satisfaction, which would consist in the repetition of a primary experience of satisfaction. (Freud, *Beyond* 36)

All appearance of progress is the elaborate deferral of a satisfaction that is lost in the past. Freud has previously identified this primary experience as an inertia (as a lump of rock is inert) and the drive toward perfection, consequently, as the wish to become 'inorganic once again' (Freud, *Beyond* 32). The inability to achieve this satisfaction, at least in life, results in a 'difference in amount between the pleasure of satisfaction which is *demanded* and that which is actually *achieved* that provides the driving factor which will permit of no halting at any position attained' (Freud, *Beyond* 36). This pressure that results from difference is desire, a force whose true object, always repressed, must be replaced by an endless series of inadequate substitutions. 'The backward path . . . is obstructed . . . so there is no alternative but to advance in the direction in which growth is still free – though with no prospect of bringing the process to a conclusion or of being able to reach the goal' (Freud, *Beyond* 36). Having discovered (if not created) this backward path, analysis mimics the activity: it advances into the analysand's past along the detour of resistance and regression. The analysand's desire for a coherent, comprehensible ego leads to a series of ostensibly ever-earlier self-representations spoken for the analyst, though in reality the speaker must create them anew. Like confession, analysis transforms a feeling of alienation, of sickness, into an account of separation; it encourages one who is lost to trust his past to a listener who will make sense of it.

The need for an authority to understand, and thereby to confirm that the transgressor was lost and is now found finds a unique expression in narrative. Jacques Lacan provides an explanation for this role for narrative through his investigations of the place of language in psychoanalytic practice, specifically in his definition of the self as 'subject' in relation to the 'discourse of the other.' The formulation of desire that Freud articulates in *Beyond the Pleasure Principle* reappears in explicitly linguistic terms in Lacan's writing. Because the 'primary experience of satisfaction' we have all at one time had remains always beyond the articulation of speech, we have no way of saying what we want. It remains forever a 'need,' the speaking of which, if it were possible, would allow us to seek, and perhaps find, our real object. Speaking it would be nearly equivalent to its satisfaction, to the *jouissance* that transcends all limits (Lacan, *Écrits* 211). However, because whatever can be announced in language (the demand) is always inadequate to the need, a gap opens between the two. The desire that arcs across that gap provides the force that prevents a speaker from ever coming to rest in a complacent approximation of the truth.

Desire makes sense only if one can imagine that some other exists who already has the desirable thing, and who might therefore provide the desiring subject with what he needs. A demand is always presented to another who may or may not respond. In Lacan's formulation, an actual response from the other is never required to sustain the sense of that other's existence: 'every speech,' Lacan writes, 'contains its own reply.' This reply arises from within the speaker's own words, but not from his conscious intention. Speaking, that is, moves one from a primal isolation into a social realm of signification that is not completely within the speaker's control. Because the limited possibilities of language determine how a demand can be expressed, the desiring subject is not fully present in his own speech. He cannot, therefore, find out who he is by questioning himself, but must seek his confirmation in the reply of another who can say, 'I know you.'

For Lacan, this sense of estrangement from one's self is implicit in the structure of the sign and the way the subject is, consequently, represented in significance. In his definition of a signifier ('there is no other'), Lacan writes:

A signifier is that which represents the subject for another signifier. This signifier will therefore be the signifier for which all the other signifiers represent the subject: that is to say, in the absence of this signifier, all the other signifiers represent nothing, since nothing is represented only *for* something else. (316)

Rather than being the foundation and source of speech, the observer of the world, and the rational discoverer of truth, the subject is 'nothing' but a locus indicated by its relation to a structure of meaning of which it is not itself a part. It is the signifier, that is, not the subject, that participates in meaning, and that signifier represents the subject only when it engages other signifiers. Consequently, any attempt to pass beyond the signifier to apprehend the unmediated subject can only lead to the vanishing of the subject or the end of speech.

Within Lacan's formulation, one cannot say that any speaker has a stable, coherent presence, that his desires, meaning, and language are his own. Introspection is a delusion, since each person has to seek his meaning through the speech of others. Confession, in this context, is an attempt to objectify the self – to present it as a knowable object – through a narrative that 're-structures' (Lacan 48) the self as history and conclusions. No matter how one's experiences may be present in memory, the events of these narratives are understandable only when they are transformed into objects for consciousness, into histories rather than sensations. It is apparently a perverseness of language that condemns each of these confessions to failure insofar as they always leave the crucial gap, the 'censored chapter' that Lacan claims for his own analysis (Lacan 50). The failure of speech to be adequate to its subject calls for exegesis; confession engenders interpretation, drawing the listener into the production of meaning.

The ontological question of self-presence, of Being, is, for western culture, a matter of life and death. In the tense paradox of our conception of individuality, to be separate from oneself is as dangerous, as deadly, as separation from the source of Being. This paradox, as I will discuss further later, develops in each infant as an almost inevitable consequence of becoming human in the western world with a western language. The advantage of conceiving of narrative as confession rather than expression is that it allows us to see the pathos of the simultaneous pursuit and evasion of meaning in narrative. It also reveals, coincidentally, the tragedy and irony implicit in the semiotic revision of psychoanalysis. Using Freud's notion of the 'memory trace' to provide a bridge to linguistic practices, Derrida writes:

Following a schema that continually guides Freud's thinking, the movement of the trace is described as an effect of life to protect itself *by deferring* the dangerous investment, by constituting a reserve. And all the conceptual oppositions that furrow Freudian thought relate each concept to the other like movements of a detour, within the economy of differance.

(Derrida, 'Differance' 150)

Life can move in only one direction, toward death, but the economy of the trace allows it to avoid the irreversible, unknowable investment in that end. Though it does not alter the end and in fact depends on death to orient desire, the effect of life is to discover all possible alternative routes. The detour is the swerving from death that is the very activity of life and of language.

There is a fertile dilemma here. The inherent inability of language to constitute *presence* itself is experienced by a speaker as alienation: we are lost from ourselves. The anxiety of that situation motivates a drive to produce oneself. But if that end were obtained, it would be tantamount to death, for such knowledge could only mean that in our individual presence, we are separate from Being. We are, in this situation, saved from ourselves by language. The mistake we inevitably make is to think of consciousness as a product of our Being rather than as an effect of loss and deferral. This error mirrors the simultaneous attainment of knowledge and sin in western mythology. In Derrida's formulation, consciousness is 'a determination and effect within a system which is no longer that of presence but that of differance' (Derrida, 'Differance' 147). Consciousness, then, is not a signified, a truth, but an effect of the displacements of differing and deferring of 'fallen' speech.

As I suggested in the discussion of Freud above, the act of confession provides a compensation in the power it establishes over another. The idea that 'consciousness' is only an 'effect' does not diminish the allure it presents to a reader: each confession appears to contain an as yet unexpressed truth to be discovered by interpretation. Consciousness is the seductive objectification of the subject, guaranteeing that the continuous deferrals of language are not babble but meaning. In a discussion of the relation between truth and knowledge in Hegel, Lacan makes the point that the subject must arouse in the other a desire to know. He defines 'truth' in Hegel's *Phenomenology* as 'that which knowledge can apprehend as knowledge only by setting its ignorance to work.' Knowledge depends upon the activity of ignorance, upon a 'state of constant re-absorption in [truth's] own disturbing element' (Lacan 296). Knowledge, that is,

11

is never more than the momentary effect of the laboring beyond the boundaries of the known, in ignorance. Truth, as ignorance, is the impossible temptation to knowledge. In setting the readers' ignorance to work, the narrator shows readers what they lack, shows them why they do not know themselves. The desire to know, then, is a response to representation: readers cannot pursue Truth directly because the path to truth depends on another who seems to represent it. It is this desire, a mediated desire, that the writer can use to gain the complicity of the reader. Truth, like Love, would no longer be Truth if it could be possessed. But whether a direct knowledge of Truth and love is forbidden, or merely impossible, the desire for them is contagious.

The possibility that this turbulent element of truth and ignorance might in fact be contagious in language – and that a reader might thereby feel himself a sinner just by reading – is supported by one of Lacan's definitions of that other turbulent element of human life, the unconscious. Lacan calls it, 'that part of the concrete discourse, insofar as it is transindividual, that is not at the disposal of the subject in re-establishing the continuity of his conscious discourse' (Lacan, *Écrits* 49). This curious definition of the 'unconscious' helps account for the power one writer's discourse can have over the language and, consequently, identities of subsequent writers. It is inside the writer as 'concrete discourse,' not as knowledge, which means it affects all language without any individual being able to control it. The formal coherence by which a writer constitutes his own consciousness does not affect the unconscious element, yet this element is what enters the discourse of the reader, infecting his language, reforming him as a subject. What is important here is that intersubjectivity is conceived of not as sympathy or understanding, but purely as an element of a shared discourse.

Intersubjectivity is not experienced, however, as discourse but as recognition, as the knowledge of something already known. Few feelings are more common (and few critical remarks more banal since Pope so succinctly formulated it) than the illusion that a writer has expressed one's own thoughts. Although the first response to a fascinating narrative may be the delight of seeing a bright verity disclosed, the more time one then spends working over the text, the more its truths seem one's own. In the activity of interpretation, a reader will almost inevitably find the text to be a confirmation of his own thoughts, both happy and fearful (or an almost personal attack on him, which amounts to the same thing). If the activity of the writer is motivated by a desire to confess his own sense of loss and desire, the reader will find himself engaged in the same motivations, though he may not recognize that the history he strives to comprehend becomes increasingly his own, not the writer's. The writer's work, in short, becomes the field on which the reader attempts to realize himself; or, as Hegel writes, 'to obtain through their action the consciousness of their unity with reality' (Hegel 234).

The most rewarding insights of reading are narcissistic. Such a conclusion would probably be denied by most readers since, as flattering as it may be to find oneself confirmed in another's text (and therein to feel one's mastery over it), that reflection also suggests one's redundancy. Such doubling indicates a discomforting lack of a unique soul in the individual and, consequently, suggests that he is secondary, replaceable. As Freud said of the uncanny double, 'from having been an assurance of immortality . . . [it] becomes the ghastly harbinger of death' (Freud, 'The "Uncanny"' 141). The reader enters into a powerful tension in interpreting a text. Because recognition (finding what one already knows) contains this threat of the uncanny, interpretation produces resistance in spite of the desire to understand. That resistance, I will argue, appears in the denial most readers will show to the idea that interpretation requires readers to become complicit with the motivations of the writer.

It is this denial that transforms the dialogue of confession into a genuine struggle for power. Because we want to see ourselves as autonomous beings constituted independently of the words we speak, we fail to recognize the limits of our ability to control or possess our own language. To a great extent, our statements contain us, not we them.

Foucault has described the relations implicit in the exchange of narrative by considering statements in their most concrete form. As an object, a statement has a place within the economy of the world. Foucault writes: 'the statement circulates, is used, disappears, allows or prevents the realization of a desire, serves or resists various interests, participates in challenge and struggle, and becomes a theme of appropriation or rivalry' (Foucault, *Archaeology* 105). It is the activity a statement generates and participates in that creates value in the statement. Despite his own sense of guilt, a confessor commands a power over a listener because he controls the material the other is obligated to use to be the one who understands.

What is startling in Foucault's description is his recognition that 'statements' are not in practice freely produced. They are limited by the cultural situation of the users. Consequently, their value is determined not by 'the presence of a secret content' but by 'their capacity for circulation and exchange, their possibility of transformation, not only in the economy of discourse, but, more generally, in the administration of scarce resources' (Foucault, *Archaeology* 120). Discourse 'poses the question of power; [it is] an asset that is, by nature, the object of a struggle, a political struggle.' The confessor can produce his place in the world only on the capital of his discourse, and thus depends on expanding his influence through a sort of imperialism of discourse.

What begins as a personal sense of sin, of alienation, has inescapable social, political, religious implications because the only possibility of attaining atonement is through the elusive medium of a narrative. And because each narrative requires interpretation, readers are drawn into the economy of a discursive exchange. Each reader, becoming a writer, recognizes the secondariness of his language, that he has only the coin that has been minted by another, not the stuff of reality, to articulate his understanding. A confessor listening cannot maintain a position outside that of a confessor speaking: secondariness is contagious. But for some readers this language, this object of exchange, begins to shape the desires of others and thereby becomes a source of power. The hopes for meaning, understanding, and atonement become allied with modes of exchange, desire, and revenge.

Much of what I have been claiming about narrative does not depart from what has been said elsewhere in psychoanalytic and semiotic studies. What I am more concerned with is the persistence which this sense of loss, a loss that seems implicit in the linguistic structure of narrative, is interpreted as a form of sin: as failure, error, inadequacy, or original damnation. The 'religious' function of narrative to reconcile the contradictory elements of existence helps to explain why we in general resist anything like a semiotic interpreta-

explain why we in general resist anything like a semiotic interpretation, and why the 'failure' of that function should produce the passions of guilt, desire, and obligation to which I have pointed. The form of confession allows me to explore the narrative response to loss in connection with the powerful metaphysical traditions of western culture. These next few paragraphs will look more directly at confession within that tradition.

In *The Symbolism of Evil* Paul Ricoeur sees the language of confession as the means of connecting a sense of guilt (unworthiness, the separation from God) to the myths of first sins. The sense of guilt can be made meaningful by introducing it into a symbolic order, transforming blind oppression into an obligation. Ricoeur recognizes that because all action in a fallen world is misdirected, perverted, it requires interpretation. 'Experience is abstract, in spite of its lifelike appearance . . . because it is separated from the totality of meaning' (Ricoeur 10). Action, like reading, produces an experience of being different, extra, that divorces the actor from the sense of totality. Any disruptive, transgressive experience, any new experience, violates that totality we call the self, so that one sees oneself simultaneously as strange, beyond familiar boundaries of comprehension, and familiar. Yet commonly, strangeness feels like guilt, and since every effect requires a cause, there must have been sin, a violation of the divine totality.

When Ricoeur speaks of the confessional re-creation of a transgressive act as sin, he identifies the original act with writing:

The experience of which the believer makes avowal in the confession of sins *creates a language* for itself by its very strangeness; the experience of being oneself but alienated from oneself gets *transcribed* immediately on the plane of language in the mode of interrogation. Sin, as alienation from oneself, is an experience more astonishing, disconcerting, and scandalous, perhaps, than the spectacle of nature.   (Ricoeur 8; my emphasis)

In its appearance as difference (as uninterpretable strangeness), the experience can be understood only as writing, not as an immediately self-disclosing nature. The experience of strangeness allows one to see oneself as both doubled and different, as inscribed in an event that can then be *transcribed*. The sense of self-unity is lost in the face of this representation of the self, and the actor asks, Who am I? What have I done? Sin, for Ricoeur, is not the transgression of a prior law, but a concept springing from the very attempt to question and explain.

This questioning itself is not subject to reflection or analysis. In the confessional situation the 'believer' submits his question to God: he locates the problem in sin, in a metaphysical rather than ontological fault. 'Sin makes me incomprehensible to myself: God is hidden; the course of things no longer has meaning.' What was known face to face is lost. In the sinner's interrogation of God, he is 'warding off meaninglessness' (Ricoeur 8). The recreation of experience as sin is revision, a *Nachträglichkeit* that attempts to establish a foundation of law and myth to account for what is strange. It gives meaning to what was 'disconcerting and scandalous' by transforming it into repetition of a mythic first sin. Ricoeur locates the means for effecting the transformation in the confession of sins, for in confession the event is reenacted in a context that reestablishes the boundaries of the violated law. Confession recalls the sinner to himself.

The importance of confession, and of the langauge of fault in general, lies in its power to interpret; but Ricoeur, like many others, does not see interpretation as an innocent activity. Sin cannot be immediately known. As he points out, the language of fault 'is itself already a hermeneutics . . .: defilement is spoken of under the symbol of a stain or blemish, sin under the symbol of missing the mark, of a tortuous road' (Ricoeur 9). Sin can be spoken of only in symbols of negation, interpreted through what is concretely present. But while the pain of loss is felt by all people, the state of being prior to sin is inconceivable except as the opposite of sin, the negation of a negation: the tortuous road has its referent in life's toils, but where is the life so free of sin that it would correspond to the straight way? So although the confessor hopes to regain his innocence by constructing a wholly comprehensible, coherent representation of himself, he must pursue his goal through the detour of negation: he can only speak of innocence by speaking of sin, reenacting in the language of confession the loss he feels.

The ambivalence of the sinner's position appears in Ricoeur's statement on the desire to interpret sin in confession.

Sin is perhaps the most important of the occasions for questioning, but also for reasoning incorrectly by giving premature answers . . . [The] unseasonable answers of gnosis and of the etiological myth testify that man's most moving experience, that of being lost as a sinner, communicates with the need to understand and excites attention by its very character as scandal.

(Ricoeur 8)

The experience of loss and the desire for answers arise together. Any answer, however, will probably come too early (premature, unseasonable), leading to a further deferral of truth. The answers do not resolve the loss or still the questioning, but deviate further from the path and perpetuate the need to confess. As Ricoeur suggests, a misguided course of reasoning may not be the only reason confessions remain unfinished: confession, by its evocation of sin, 'excites attention,' drawing one to it rather than ushering one to a purged conclusion. The use of the word 'scandal' suggests its etymological roots as a trap and snare, so that the one who has been snared by sin becomes in turn the scandalous trap. The one hearing the confession, once his attention has been excited, is himself involved in the need to understand. But in the attempt to explain, the interpreter himself strays, 'reasoning incorrectly,' providing 'premature answers' that in turn demand a further interpretation to return to right reason, to read the mature answer that has been deferred. The confessing sinner is thus both penitent and tempter. Confession, through the reenactment of sin, sins again, even to the point of drawing the listener into interpretations that inevitably have their own strayings. To become involved with a confession is to experience oneself the alienation motivating the speaker, and thereby to be thrust onto confession's long detour back to a primal state of innocence.

The readings in the following chapters demonstrate the variety of genres and periods that seem to manifest the contending motivations of desire and obligation. The three shorter 'exemplary readings' below are meant to display the method and possibilities of 'confessional' readings. The different kinds of confessions and the very different confessors also provide a practical definition of the basic terms of this argument. Just as this introduction has been less a marshalling of philosophic support than a reading of a tradition, the following chapters will not reveal the enduring presence of a previously undetected truth underlying all literature; rather, it demonstrates an involvement in the processes it examines, demonstrates that reading is complicit in the motivations of writing.

The longer treatments of *The Scarlet Letter*, *Absalom, Absalom!*, and *The Unnamable* that follow work through the issues of this introduction. These texts are deeply set in the problem of discourse and power: the narrator of the Custom House, Quentin Compson, and the voice of *The Unnamable* have always been aware of the terrible, heroic ancestors and madmen, or merely Beckett's *them*, who have condemned the narrators to live within their histories. The three are all readers, belated progeny of the great narrators, and all narrate to free themselves by appropriating the dominating voices. My interest is in how each goes about fulfilling his obligation. Hawthorne recasts his ancestors' language of government and theology in a story of repressed passion that systematically confuses the languages of sexuality and religion. In *The Unnamable* the narrator takes such traditions as theology, philosophy, and literature, that he is heir to and victim of, and he weaves them into his own endless discourse, exposing and mocking the dualisms on which the traditions are founded. And Quentin uses the narrative of Sutpen that he has known from birth to try to assume control of his own distraught life as a son and brother, submitting the authority of history to the disrupting intrusions of miscegenation and incest.

None of these texts is traditionally confessional, but that is part of my point. The confessional tradition informs the workings of many kinds of narrative, the significant feature being that they are narrated by characters consumed with guilt and driven to talk about it. This narrative situation is disarming: when is one more truthful than when confessing? to what does one listen with a more sympathetic willingness to understand than a confession? But it is precisely through the exploitation of common sense and common sympathy, which are nothing less than the languages we use without thinking, that these books find the faults in us that turn virtuous readers into complicit confessors. They exploit what Beckett calls 'impotence,' which means to exploit the readers' reliance on a dualism of being and non-being, I and not-I, that structures the language, much as St Augustine and Dimmesdale could be said to exploit sin in a culture that divided existence along lines of the redeemed and the damned, or Faulkner to exploit 'miscegenation' in a land where the division into white and non-white is so absolute that pale, thin-lipped 'octoroons' are still 'niggers.' These writers systematically disrupt the distinctions their readers require in order fully to understand, even though they claim that the distinctions are vitally important. The contradiction forces the reader into an interpretive dilemma: the desire to resolve the confusion is aroused while the means to resolve it are undermined.

By taking their readers through this dilemma, these books offer the possibility of refusing *understanding* (the mastery of meaning) as a purpose of narrative. The writers pose as masters of their texts, but only to disclose finally the illusory nature of the category, for both writers and readers. For is it only the desire for a masterful author that makes one into a slavish reader.

2
Three exemplary readings

The endless confession

About ten years after his conversion in 386, Augustine wrote his *Confessions*, a statement of faith and devotion to his God. He was at that time Bishop of Hippo, a position of such authority and prominence that his faith could not be a matter of public question. The decision to publish an account of his life under these circumstances suggests the presence of a lingering uneasiness that his position has not allayed. In the opening pages he writes, 'The thought of you [God] stirs [man] so deeply that he cannot be content unless he praises you, because you made us for yourself and our hearts find no place until they rest in you' (C 21). The book is formally addressed to God by a writer desiring, and so presumably lacking, a sense of his place. the act of prayer, however, settles the stirred man, gathering and locating his essential self in God. Only in addressing himself to God does Augustine know himself. But in the very existence of the *Confessions* as a published work, a division arises in the book's addressee, one that Augustine recognizes: 'Why, then, does it matter to me whether men should hear what I have to confess, as though it were they who were to cure all the evil that is in me?' (C 208). Yet it does matter to him. Although the book may be a prayer to God, it is written to be read by mortals. Perhaps readers can cure his uneasiness, but to do so they must anchor the writer's vagrant heart. Augustine's double audience with its division between human and divine realms provides a source of tension in the *Confessions*.

A confession to an omniscient diety, after all, cannot tell the auditor anything new. This situation conditions the narrative in ways Augustine was aware of: 'If a man confesses to you, he does not reveal his inmost thoughts to you as though you did not know them' (C 91). The confession is a 'sacrifice,' a ritual performance, a statement whose purpose is not to represent some event but to enact a relationship between God and man; and yet it is performed for men curious for stories. Augustine claims, however, that he evokes a response in his reader beyond mere curiosity about his sins. 'Their hearts are roused by the love of your mercy and the joy of your grace' (C 208) because Augustine allows them to see in him a model for their own lives within a pattern of sin and redemption. Those who had despaired of their sins can see in Augustine's salvation the possibility of their own. The effect of the book depends on readers' coming to interpret their own lives in terms provided by Augustine, reading his history to understand theirs.

Frequently Augustine speaks of a personal self-reflexive purpose in the writing. Without forgetting the reader who follows his history, he suggests that the act of writing itself affects the writer immediately. 'Let me know you, for you are the God who knows me' (C 207), he writes at the opening of Book X. Although much of his confession narrates the process of coming to know himself, he implies that he comes to know God by writing his own history: that is, by confessing he comes to know God, to know himself as God does, ultimately to share the divine perspective. His presentation of himself in confession constitutes the aspect of God that he can understand. Although the prayer here is to know God, this construction unsettles the relationship between God and man both by making God resemble Augustine and by allowing Augustine to aspire toward a godly vision. In any event, Augustine's sense of himself as an object of God's knowledge coincides with his self-representation as a sinner.

It is not clear here what it would mean to know God, nor are the motives for desiring that knowledge straightforward, especially considered in light of the 'secondary' addressee, the reader. As early as the incident of his stealing pears in Book II (C 51), Augustine reveals that frequently before his conversion he acted principally to achieve some effect on others – in this case to impress his friends with his willingness to join in their petty crime – and has never ceased in succeeding years to enjoy the admiration that his brilliance could inspire. The goals of his performances (the pears for the child, the demonstration of a powerful rhetoric for the adult) were displacements of his desire to surpass those he admired. He discovers through such experiences the power mimetic desire could have over him, a knowledge he then employs to affect others. He gives an example of how mimetic desire led him toward conversion. When he was near his own conversion and yet still unwilling to make the necessary joint 'act of will' and profession of faith, Simplicianus, 'spiritual father Ambrose,' tells him of Victorinus. Offered the option of professing his faith in private, Victorinus 'preferred to declare his salvation in full sight of the assembled faithful' (C 161). The result is that the 'hushed voices of the whole exultant congregation joined in the murmur "Victorinus, Victorinus,"' something Victorinus, master of rhetoric, could hardly have failed to anticipate. Although Augustine follows this with references to the lost sheep that is found and to the prodigal son delighting the father with his return, he, also a master of rhetoric, could not have missed the suggestion in Simplicianus's sly simplicity that Augustine, were he only to convert, would also hear his name murmured in a hundred mouths. Simplicianus implies that Augustine would not only be like Victorinus, but would also be imitating Ambrose, Victorinus's imitator and Augustine's model. The form of public confession closely resembles the young Augustine's proud display of rhetoric and suggests that under a guise of piety the desire for admiration continues unchanged. It is this desire Augustine can use to seduce his readers.

I am not suggesting Augustine is merely vain, but that he desires, like Simplicianus, to prompt his readers to imitate his own conversion. He would still lead readers to recognize God's mercy, but along *his* path because they admire *him*. From such admiration Augustine would derive a confirmation of his own confession, both that he was a sinner and that he is now redeemed, just as admiration confirmed the rhetorician's skill. Consequently, the comfort Augustine claims to derive from God through confession depends on a reader, an other able to confirm his confession as a confession by replying. In the opening paragraph of Book I just preceding the passage quoted above, Augustine reveals the crucial motive for confessing: 'Man is one of your creatures, Lord, and his instinct is to praise you. He bears about him the mark of death, the sign of his sin, to remind him that you "thwart the proud"' (C 21). In the apposition of death with 'the sign of his sin,' Augustine draws an equivalence between the two that removes death from mere contingency and gives it meaning. Death is the ultimately determining event, the sign of separation from God and hence of God's presence, hidden from man by his sins. The desire to overcome the sense of separation from God is, then, a motivation for confession, but at the same time confession will continually recall the mark of death. To expiate the sin prior to meeting

God face to face would mean one loses the most evident sign of His reality.

Confession generates its own motivation, reassuring the confessor of his eventual return to God through a perpetual recounting of his situation as alienated sinner. But the confirmation of this alienation, the legitimizing of the sin as sin, can derive only from the normative understanding of his readers. He weaves his narrative from the common narrative of sin, and thus he can be assured of his readers' response, that they will thrill or recoil at the enormities of the young man and will sympathize with Augustine's joy at the possibility of redemption. The remarkable Augustine plays out the patterns of the common man, reading his own sins so that his readers can follow the path with a sense of familiarity. Sin requires recognition, and the best recognition is the mirror of imitation.

The relation between rhetoric and seduction appears again as Augustine begins his final turn toward Christianity, at the point where he falls under the rhetorical power of Ambrose. He listens closely to Ambrose 'to judge . . . whether the reports of his powers as a speaker were accurate . . . So while I pay the closest attention to the words he used, I was quite uninterested in the subject matter' (C 107). Yet it is precisely through this attention to the surface of the talk that Augustine begins reading properly (the central fact of his conversion) and then repeating the forms and techniques Ambrose applied. Ambrose reads with a theory of figural interpretation based not on full, literal speech, on a present referent, but on the inevitable absence of the divine. The consequent disjunction between words and referents, signifiers and signifieds, prevents Augustine from ever mastering Ambrose's subject. Listening, he follows an endlessly deferred meaning. Paying 'the closest attention to the words,' Augustine learns figures, not meanings, and thus in his desire to attain Ambrose's authority he identifies his new spiritual life with Ambrose's theological discourse. Ambrose's technique becomes that of Augustine's own *Confessions*.

The movement of the *Confessions* displays this strategy of deferral and imitation. Augustine, alluring confessor, moves alternately toward transgression and toward redemption, playing out a narrative that involves the reader in precisely the form of interpretation and repetition Augustine learned from Ambrose, while the reader need consciously attend to only the surface development of the tale. The narrative proceeds through dozens of delays, trials of understanding that repeatedly fail against the dead end of the Manichean's materialistic dualism. And at every failure Augustine says he was 'not yet' ready, and lapses into prayer. The unquestioned conviction of a Christian era that a final solution is possible provides an ideological ground for these deferrals: failure is never a sign to the reader that an authoritative reading is a delusion, but, rather, it is the mark of Augustine's lingering difference from God. With such an idea of difference, each failed resolution points toward perfection at the same time it denies the very possibility of attaining that state, renewing the desire for the concluding mystery of conversion at the same time as it is deferred for another book.[1] Insofar as sin is a separation from God – from truth, authority, finality – Augustine situates his reader in the allegorical equivalent of sin. Desiring the truth of conversion, the knowledge that led Augustine to God, the reader enacts Augustine's separation, acknowledging in every interpretive movement that he does not yet know how to return to grace. He becomes involved in the narrative as a sinner and consequently must (or so Augustine would hope) continue to read and interpret Augustine, depending on Augustine to lead him out of sin again.

This pattern of repeating and extending the discourse, rather than presenting clearly the course of conversion and the discovered truths of God, is displayed powerfully in the larger structure of the text. Considering that throughout the first half of the *Confessions* Augustine repeatedly suggests that the impediment to his conversion lay in his not yet having comprehended the true nature of God or the proper way of reading his Word, it is curious that when his collapse beneath the fig tree occurs, he has not yet explained how he reached this state. The narrative is emotional and highly poetic at this point (resembling in this sense Socrates's moment of revelation with Diotima in the *Symposium*), abandoning the show of rational exploration that dominates much of Augustine's writing. Significantly, the conversion occurs less than half-way through the book. This moment has been typically viewed as the end of the 'confession proper,'[2] at which point the gap between the man narrating and the subject of the narration closes: Augustine has revealed himself; the narrative is over. Yet quite obviously the *Confessions* continues. What follows the event encompasses and extends the pattern of confession that has preceded; in other words, Augustine is his own first reader.[3]

24

Augustine continues interpreting, but the topic turns away from his personal history. Increasingly it is the writer, not the sinner, we attend to. In the Book succeeding the conversion, he briefly narrates the story of his mother, Monica: 'I will omit not a word that my mind can bring to birth concerning your servant, my mother. In the flesh she brought me to birth in this world' (C 192). It is a tribute to Monica, but in these mutual births is an echo of another passage I have quoted ('Let me know you, for you are the God who knows me,' [C 207]) as part of Augustine's reason for writing. He narrates Monica's conversion, then, not simply to glorify her, but to reenter the interpretive path that produced him. The incestuous image of birth, in which Augustine brings forth his own mother, suggests that the offspring would be at least half Augustine.

The story he then tells is another of sin and conversion, including interpretations of that conversion that occurred in conversations between mother and son. Augustine says of these conversations, 'This [interpretation] was the purpose of our talk, though we did not speak in precisely these words or exactly as I have reported them' (C 198). Conversion and conversation are both, apparently, matters of interpretive revision for Augustine, requiring one to find in the overly earthy stories of mothers and Biblical parables traces of the transcendent. His speech joins mother and son as it does God and sinner. He brings forth a story of his mother that resembles his own, basing it on an interpretation of her life that he helped to develop and that he has recast in his own terms. As accurate as the details may be, Augustine has nevertheless appropriated her history to his own narrative, reworking it in his image. Monica's last request is that Augustine 'remember [her] at the altar of the Lord' (C 199). Just as silent prayer is insufficient as a medium of Augustine's confession, it is inadequate to acknowledge Monica, and so he incorporates her into his text: 'So it shall be that the last request my mother made to me shall be granted in the prayers of the many who read my confessions more fully than in mine alone' (C 105). Monica could be 'remembered' by the *many* readers who repeat her narrative, once while reading and again when they pray for her, remembering Augustine's words. Because he has inscribed her story within his text, each prayer would necessarily rehearse the *Confessions*. What is important here is not that he may have abused Monica's tale, but that he made of her a textual object that requires the reader to remember and repeat it and to return, therefore,

25

to the text of the *Confessions*. Her story has repeated Augustine's in small, but has brought the reader no nearer to an understanding of Augustine's conversion.

Augustine does not, however, abandon the task of interpretation to his reader's talents at this point. He still claims to wish to know himself as he is (toward the end of knowing God) and he supposes, by the way, that those who have taken an interest in him thus far might want to read more. What follows is the meditation on memory and the action of the mind, while the actions of the man in the world are set aside. Augustine seems here to have come to a problem John Freccero has noted: how does Augustine connect the errant youth with the magisterial philosopher? Freccero writes: 'Conversion demands that there be both continuity and discontinuity between the self that *is* and the self that was; similarly, a narrative of the self demands that author and persona be distinguished until they are fused at the culminating moment' (Freccero 36). The self that is, like the idea of an author, remains inevitably beyond representation, remains a site of full presence that would need no representational substitute. It is only the self that was, the representable persona that promises the eventual emergence of an authorial master. As Freccero points out, this culminating moment cannot occur in the text, but only through a transcendent deity in which signifier and signified find their point of identity. To suggest that this moment could occur in the text is, in Freccero's terms, idolatry, the reification of the sign, the end of referentiality. Augustine has reported a conversion, but the event happens within a flood of tears, and the new man has been born. His task then is to demonstrate the continuity of the essential Augustine not only from sinner to saved man, but on to him who writes the confession, and he seeks this continuity through a dialectic that carries forward and repeats his past.

Although the reply to the question 'Who am I?' does not directly address the events of the first part, it does return to examine the way they were represented, interpreting and justifying the entire project of the confession. Augustine has explained his need to recount his sins: 'For love of your love I shall retrace my wicked ways' (C 43). His first, and perhaps most intense perception of God's love occurs at the moment of conversion, in the transition from alienation to acceptance. While the retracing may be the method of effacing the sin and achieving forgiveness, it explicitly takes the confessor back through the sin, mentally and emotionally reenacting the process that brought him to the point of conversion. But there seems to be something more here. Much of what Augustine says about the status of mental activities suggests that to retrace is to sin again, with sin's pleasures and griefs. He makes it clear that the mental reenactment is equivalent to the physical deed insofar as they equally define his identity. He says that in thinking of 'things,' of events and tangible objects, his memory will provide him with images for them, but memory has no images for 'facts' and abstractions, and God, as he has made clear, has no image-able body. Of intangibles he says: 'If, for a short space of time, I cease to give them my attention, they sink back and recede again into the remote cell of my memory, so that I have to think them out again, like a fresh set of facts, if I am to know them' (C 218). But he is himself such a vanishing fact. The 'self that is' is only the culminations of past selves and thus needs constant remembering to exist as more than a thing. His argument comes down to the necessity 'to think out again,' to interpret and repeat whatever one would know. The retracing of his sins, then, is not so much the compensation for the gap that has opened between the vanished sinner and the reborn saint. Instead it is the act which locates Augustine as the writer of the *Confessions*: St Augustine is he who remembers the past, not as accident, but as sin.

For Augustine, man in himself is mind, and mind is always a present attention to some object moving between expectation and memory. He comments on 'history': 'When we describe the past correctly, it is not past facts which are drawn out of our memories but only words based on our memory-pictures of these facts' (C 267). Words are different from the events they refer to ('generally inaccurate and seldom complete,'[C 269]), but as objects of attention, their failure to be literal – i.e., word equivalent to thing – is unimportant. As attention moves through a text it is continually gathering the remembered beginning and the anticipated end, and it interprets the word he is reading at the moment in the light of this gathering. He demonstrates this process with the example of a psalm recited from memory: at first the psalm is all expectation, and as he recites, i.e., gives his attention to particular lines, the psalm is regathered as memory. From this textual model, he goes on to generalize: 'What is true of the whole psalm is also true of its parts . . . It is true of a man's whole life, of which all his actions are parts' (C 278). A man's life has coherence and meaning, like a poem. And to be recited, of course, the life must be written.

Augustine finds himself caught here between the desire to produce a stable text of his life that will recreate him with every repetition, and the inevitable instability (due to the inaccuracy of words) that is the consequence of each reader's interpretation. To escape the dilemma, he makes an important qualification: to read properly one must read with 'charity' (C 302): love of God and man will inform reading with truth. He must recognize, however, that before his conversion, he read critically, not charitably, despite his desire to know the truth, and that others are likely to also. Only the most normative of readers would understand him as he wishes to be, but only the deviant reader will do the work necessary to 'think out' again the text's implications. He cannot therefore hope that any consistent meaning will be discovered by his readers; what he can hope for is that they will imitate his reading, that he can make charity a matter method.

At the end of the book, Augustine shifts his focus once again even further away from the ephemeral self that had occupied the previous segments and begins demonstrating his readings of the Bible. Much earlier, Augustine had acquired some 'Platonist' works. 'In them I read – not, of course, word for word, though the sense was the same – . . . *that at the beginning of time the Word already was*' (C 144), and several pages of quotation from the Bible follow. Augustine, in a demonstration of charity in reading, appropriates the discourse of Christianity's most potent rival for his own purposes. We should expect the same strong readings when he turns to the Bible. He once again faces a text that deviates from literal truth ('These passages had been death to me when I took them literally' [C 108]) as he had faced the text of his own life's deviation from God's path and the death that had been the 'mark of sin.' In reading his life, he found that his own sins revealed God's truth through their error.

The problem he encounters reading Holy Scripture is one common to the Platonic world, as familiar to Renaissance love poetry as to structural semiotics. Sidney, for example, laments, 'What may words say, or what may words not say,/ Where Truth itself must speak like Flattery?' (*Astrophel and Stella* 35). One has only familiar words to describe this unique love, this Stella, only the relations between signs and not the one word that can present a transcendent meaning. Augustine encounters the problem when trying to imagine what is meant by the words saying the earth was 'invisible and without form': 'How, then, could it be described in such a way that even dull minds could grasp it, except by means of some familiar word?' (C 282). The words are literally inadequate, yet by exposing their own inadequacy, by violating the strictures of sense, of referentiality, they point to a meaning beyond the limited world of total comprehension. 'We must,' he says, 'be content to know without knowing, or should I say, to be ignorant and yet to know?' (C 283). This is not, however, the disadvantage it has seemed to some later writers who see it leading to an 'antiliterary' impulse, and finally silence. Augustine takes this failure of the literal as the occasion for continuous interpretation, limited only by the readers' charity.

How can it harm me that it should be possible to interpret these words in several ways, all of which may yet be true? . . . Provided therefore, that each of us tries the best he can to understand in the Holy Scriptures what the writer meant by them, what harm is there if a reader believes what you, the Light of all truthful minds, show him to be the true meaning? It may not even be the meaning which the writer had in mind, and yet he too saw in them a true meaning, different though it may have been from this.(C 296)

One cannot determine whether the text is a fullness from which many truths can be drawn, or an emptiness that will accept many truths. I suspect that for Augustine it is neither, since 'truth' is not in any given statement but in the inspiration of God, and the text, therefore, is only (but crucially) the occasion for reading and thus for inspiration to occur.

What Augustine has done is to apply the same principles of reading to the Bible that he applies to his life, taking the holy text as yet another opportunity for confessing. But he has not forgotten his public audiences:

For my part I declare resolutely and with all my heart that if I were called upon to write a book which was to be vested with the highest authority, I should prefer to write it in such a way that a reader could find re-echoed in my words whatever truths he was able to apprehend.   (C 308)

He has written such a book in his *Confessions*. It is both the text to be read and the model for its own reading and interpretive rewriting. He has by this last quotation abandoned any demand for a univocal meaning and substituted an undecidable text whose effect is to provide a topic for his reader's thought. This makes every interpretation, however, another 're-echoing' of Augustine's text. God's

29

authoritative Word made the human mind in His likeness (C 345): Augustine's project is finally to do no less. But in place of the Word and its truth, he employs the forms of interpretive thought that will be retraced and learned by anyone who reads his book. Under the guise of being God's servant, he attempts to achieve a god-like power of creation. With the initial lures of piety and scandal, Augustine leads his readers into a text that transforms the naive reader into an Augustinian reader and, often, writer. His text throughout the last two books begins to merge with the Bible, so that the reader is led from the thrilling reading of a rake's progress into the endless task of Biblical exegesis. Under the impulse of a sentiment that seems wholly religious, the reader continues the Augustinian project, sustaining Augustine as confessor through the application of Augustine's own confessional method.

A paradigm of passion

> I do this, my God, not because I love those sins, but so that I may love you. For love of your love I shall retrace my wicked way.
>
> Augustine, *Confessions*

Kierkegaard's *Diary of a Seducer*[4] falls within the tradition of the 'found' text, as does *The Scarlet Letter*, the subject of a later chapter. The 'diary' proper is stolen by 'A,' whose papers in turn have been discovered by editor Victor Eremita, who has included them in the text *Either/Or*. *Diary of a Seducer* is 'A's' 'fair copy' of the diary. From the beginning, this series of displacements unsettles the relationship of the reader to the text: it casts doubt on the origin and authority of the various transcriptions and overruns the formal limits of the text. Authors and imitators, writers and readers are doubled and concealed within the 'editions' of the text. Yet one element runs consistently through each edition, based not on the details of the story but on a pattern of seduction. To seduce Cordelia, Johannes clothes himself in the conventional language of erotic love, a strategy that works in part by undermining her sense of self-sufficiency. He then records this seduction in that same appealing, subverting language, producing a story that entraps the eavesdropping 'A,' who reads it, transcribes it, and subsequently produces his own seductive text.

Although the next few pages will develop the pattern of seduction that Johannes exploits, the truly confessional nature of the narrative only emerges in 'A's' response, the only text we have. Johannes is imagined beyond the reach of guilt, a Satanic figure whose transgression has a horrifying absoluteness to it that 'A' emulates in spite of himself, though he never matches it. 'A,' in his own guilty desire, must appropriate Johannes and create him as the authority that can interpret his own faults. Through 'A's' confessional interpretation, a world of guilt and promise passes from writer to reader, seducer to seduced, with each repetition. Each communicates a passion that exists formally only as a paradigm for representation, a contagion each lover can spread that undermines the solidarity of the world. First, Johannes's tale.

The account that the seducer Johannes gives of his affair with Cordelia dwells for the most part on the 'dance' Johannes claims to choreograph. The dance is a language of understatement in which a careless nod on a stairway, a side glance on the avenue, and the arrangement of chairs become significant. Conversation is only one form of the dance. These events, however, which could be considered the primary history of the affair, take on their full meaning only when they have been revised in Johannes's evening's journal entry. For example, early in his pursuit of Cordelia Johannes tries the effect of his 'side-glance' on her and, when she fails to respond, turns his eye on the girl's footman who stumbles: 'Yes, now you see the consequences of going out alone with a servant. He has fallen down' (Diary 20), presumably from the force of the look. Since it is unlikely that Johannes would imagine he literally possesses a supernatural gaze capable of knocking over a footman if it fails to catch-up a girl, the footman's slip has no meaning until the diary has created it. This is not to suggest that Johannes is the merely 'unreliable narrator,' altering true events to fit his own purposes, for Johannes stalks the streets collecting the accidental observations of the day for his diary: no true story underlies his diary, no intention guides his walks until he writes of it.

Although Johannes loses sight of Cordelia for a long period following the onset of his infatuation with her, it is not because she is so hard to locate. Rather, the desultory course of his search betrays a deliberate neglect of system. He prefers to let accident guide him and provide details free of any vulgar intentions on his part. Events are thus stripped from their place in the daily world and rearranged according to Love's designs: delay does not mean that they simply haven't crossed paths, but that their love has some impediment, which, naturally, inflames his desire; the fortuitous meeting when it finally occurs must then be fate, not chance. His daily walks, ostensibly intended to discover Cordelia once more, are directed less toward Cordelia than toward providing material for erotic evenings of diary entries.

What appears here in the most trivial example is more obvious in the later stages of the affair. Johannes comments: 'Some [men] are virtuous by day and sin at night, I am dissimulation by day, at night I am all desire' (Diary 69). This is, conventionally, the art of love: the lover hides his true feelings until under the cover of darkness. But Johannes remains alone at night, delaying any possibility of confessing his love, while he recreates his desire as diary. Although his daily dissimulations might be prompted by decorum, he is excited by his own doubleness, by the apparent escape from a simple determinacy. He is no longer a mere person, but a character who requires interpretation to be understood. He sees himself in terms of stories, myths, and commentaries, comparing himself at one point to Scheherazade who 'staved off the execution of the death sentence with her storytelling' (Diary 153). To be 'all desire,' it seems, is to be both the teller and the tale, the meaning behind the meaning.

To seduce and evade, he employs 'amphibolies': 'To fool them in the course of the narration, that is my pleasure' (Diary 90). These ambiguities are not, however, a common deceit, presenting one face so that another, truer face remains undetected. Johannes's amphibolies have, in fact, only the obvious first meaning, one that a listener will suddenly realize is fallacious. But there is nothing behind: the indeterminacy of Johannes's language opens a void, the lack of meaning in language. Rather than face that blank, Johannes's readers project a meaning into it. Cordelia, interpreting his speech under the pressure of her own conventional desires, naturally detects love. Johannes realizes that it is the 'secretiveness with which I manage everything' (Diary 105) that draws her attention and desire: it is not by revealing himself but by absenting himself that he becomes the object of that desire. And drawing on her desire, he retreats to his study to write.

Johannes supposes 'some will say that I have never really been in love' (Diary 64), a statement similar to the moment in *Civilization and Its Discontents* when Freud confesses his inexperience of the 'oceanic feeling' (12). Readers who dwell on billowy seas take Freud's admission as the key to his failure: if Freud has not *felt* this, how can he write about it? For Freud, however, feeling itself is the problem because it conveys so powerfully the illusion of an unmediated, authentic knowledge. His readers' inability to recognize the oceanic as a vast narcissism, of which being-in-love is one manifestation, provides the motive and force for the text. Freud is not concerned with love or God per se, but with the repetition of imagery and metaphors in descriptions of love, religious ecstasy, and intoxication of all sorts that produce the feeling. The source of the oceanic feeling cannot therefore be true love or God's grace; on the contrary, love and God appear to be the reifications of a narcissistic pleasure, part of attempts to explain, and justify, the often dangerous pleasure experienced at certain moments. They take on their particular aspects from the discourses they exist within, not from a prior being. Johannes feels pleasure, certainly, but can it be 'real love' when it is always the product of the language of love? Johannes's power over others derives from his recognition that the language itself will produce pleasure in his listener, who will experience it as love.

Johannes can depend on his listener's desire for love to find love in his words. When he does make his declaration of love, he does not speak from the heart, but like a book:

At times, however, it is quite appropriate to speak that way, for a book has the remarkable quality that it can be interpreted at will . . . It cannot be denied that she was as surprised as I had expected her to be. To describe just how she looked is difficult. Her expressions were manifold, rather like the promised, but still unpublished, commentary to my book, a commentary that will lend itself to every possible interpretation.   (Diary 96)

Whether or not Johannes is truly in-love becomes irrelevant beside the fact that this bookish show of love is capable of evoking the response he desires. Although Cordelia may have been swept away by the ambiguous love-talk, Johannes sees only a commentary, one that, being no more definitive than the original text, will itself demand further commentary. This supplement to his book is the surest sign for him of success.

The title of Johannes's manuscript, *Commentarius Perpetuus No. 4*, helps clarify the relationship between seduction and diary-keeping. The point of a seduction is to have one's love returned, and if one loves by the book, the only true return is a commentary, the perpetuation of a discourse. Commentary, in this sense, represents Johannes's possession of his lover more completely than any possession of a body. Innocent Cordelia's 'commentary' imitates the pattern of being-in-love Johannes taught her, and the diary commenting in turn on her love represents Johannes's thrill at that display of fidelity. The narcissistic pleasure of seeing his bookish representation of love mirrored for him in Cordelia inspires him to write of love. Without ever experiencing real love, he still represents it with an accuracy that calls forth recognition from one who can feel it. Having mastered the language of being-in-love, Johannes can count on every properly phrased confession of love to draw its reciprocating commentary.

It is not only the jaded Johannes whose passion is narcissistic; he is simply more aware of the nature of passion and is, consequently, more able to exploit it. 'I am creating for myself a heart in the likeness of her own,' Johannes writes (Diary 113). The object of love that Johannes presents to Cordelia is a representation of herself that appears as another. That which was Cordelia becomes a part of Johannes, which Cordelia then loves. She takes him for the original of a knowledge she has in fact already known. When he teaches her the ways of love, he only teaches her 'again and again what I have learned from her' (Diary 115). So by looking at Johannes, Cordelia is educated and charmed by an image she does not even recognize as her own. In this confirmation of the Petrarchan conceit that finds the eyes simultaneously windows and mirrors to the heart, Johannes seduces Cordelia to an unwittingly narcissistic passion.

The thrill that runs through the diary arises from Johannes's almost voyeuristic observation of the passion. He never confuses the heart he 'creates for himself' with his own. But the fact that the object of Cordelia's desire is not Johannes himself but her own image seen in him does not cool but, rather, increases his ardor. He recognizes that consummation, the oceanic interfusion of hearts, would be the 'death sentence' for his passion. Like Scheherazade, he can evade with that sentence because he knows that the end of any story is merely a convention of narrative form, ultimately as unsatisfying as sexual consummation must be to one who desires true love. His own heart is always another's that beats in response to his words. He sees himself in the drama of love as a structure of passion, not as a person:

as she learns to love, she learns to love me; as she develops the rule, the paradigm is gradually revealed, and this is myself. As through love she becomes aware of her full significance, she will devote it to loving me, and

34

when she senses that she has learned this from me, she will love me twice as much. The thought of my joy so overwhelms me that I nearly lose my cool detachment. (Diary 100)

His self lacks content. He exists only in the repetition of the 'paradigm' of love. That he is not himself the object of desire is irrelevant since the object is only virtual, an illusion emanating from within his own refracting language. What he requires for his joy, is the other to respond with the desire that will motivate further manifestations of the paradigm. He refers, in a similar moment of pleasure, to the 'life principle' (Diary 125) of his activity that is manifested in the 'simultaneity' of his and Cordelia's words in their conversations. In these conversations, the words exchanged are insignificant, for their passion contains an 'intersubjective' element that is spoken not in particular words but in the form of the exchange. Their passion must remain unobjectified in either language or bodies. For Johannes, the literalization of his passion in consummation would destroy his interest. Bodies respond less effectively than words.

Johannes the lover is not quite identical to Johannes the diarist. 'I am a myth about myself' (Diary 179), he writes as he hurries to his treacherous rendezvous with the girl. The 'myself,' the bumbling villain the seducer would appear to be to others, never emerges from behind the 'I' of myth who is transfigured by the power of love. Hence the meeting with Cordelia is not described, for that would be mere flesh, devoid of the intersubjective 'simultaneity' that characterizes the confessional relation of the two. The myth reaches its ecstatic climax, and the mythologizer continues his *Commentarius perpetuus*, reflecting upon preceding pages and proposing the direction the narrative might take in 'a fascinating epilogue': 'There is one thing, however, it would be worthwhile to know: is it possible to abandon a girl in such a way that she would imagine proudly that it was she who was breaking off the relationship because she had grown tired of it all?' (Diary 181). He wonders, in other words, whether he could instill in another the arts of seduction and mythologizing, could have his victim fulfill his paradigm to the extent that she would practice it on her own subsequent lover. This is no mere wish for aesthetic and emotional tidiness, for a convenient conclusion to the affair where no one is hurt. Its success would imply that Cordelia begins to see herself not as an object but as the myth about herself, in which case she also would require the response of a listener. She would leave him, as he leaves her, because she desires not the other's self, but his desire. Cordelia, then, would become his means of extending his 'paradigm,' much as the diary extends it to a later reader.

'A,' that hapless reader, is acquainted with both Cordelia and Johannes. He steals the manuscript from an escritoire Johannes 'customarily' locks, but for some reason ('A' has no suspicions) has left open that day. Johannes had told 'A' of his preoccupation with Cordelia, so the seed of curiosity had been planted in the snooping confidante. Cordelia, recognizing his interest, gives him a complementary bundle of passionate letters intended for (but returned by) Johannes. Whenever she would talk to 'A' about Johannes, she would recite a verse 'which seemed to mean something different according to her mood and the different way this mood induced her to recite:

> 'Gehe,
> Verschmähe
> Die Treue,
> Die Reue
> Kommt nach.'   (Diary 11)

The poem, he says, is ambiguous; her letters, lacking 'clearness,' convey 'mood' rather than 'meaning.' Their lack of definiteness and conclusion compel 'A' to provide the meaning she omits. Between the hints of passion and betrayal in Johannes's conversation and the enticing vagueness of Cordelia's letters and poem, the two seem to have joined to arouse the sharpest desire in 'A' to read the diary.

At the opening of the preface, 'A' is making a 'fair copy' of the rough transcript he had made in secret haste: 'The situation fills me with the same alarm and self-reproach I felt then' (Diary 1). The 'same': the trembling anticipation of gaining the diary, the fear of discovery, and the guilt at betraying his friend are all called back by the act of transcribing, yet it is not dismay but pleasure he derives from the repetition of his crime. His 'admiration' for Johannes's skill is superseded by his 'satisfaction' in discovering the exact form of the seducer's depravity. He compares himself to a police officer entering a forger's room, but lacking a police badge, he is also an illegitimate copyist, forging the dissembler's work. He desires to enter Johannes's world of deceit and self-consciousness, 'that nebulous, that

36

dream world where constantly one is afraid of one's own shadow' (Diary 9). And he accomplishes this through the repetition afforded by the diary.

Repetition with its attendant renewal of transgression and desire dominates 'A's' preface. His remarks on Cordelia suggest that Johannes was at least partially successful in instilling the paradigm in Cordelia. He comments that Johannes 'has wakened many-tongued reflection within her' (Diary 8). The sleep of innocence allows one the illusion of self-coherence, of desire directed unambiguously toward its object. But the awakening is the recognition that she is not only not a coherent, single being, but she is incomplete besides. The 'many-tongued reflection' is that internal babble of competing voices, and it is also those images of one's missing self, the other parts each of us has had to suppress in order to be who we are, the half Aristophanes speaks of in the *Symposium*. But since no actual object can be that half, no legitimate possession will fulfill Cordelia's desire. What Johannes promises is something beyond, but like all such promises, it says that it can be fulfilled only by overstepping boundaries. The guilt arising from her transgressions, however, does not serve to restrain her. Rather, the guilt acts as a goad to memory, taking her thoughts back to him: 'Then memory awakens in her soul, she forgets the fault and the guilt, she remembers the beautiful moments, and she is swayed by an unnatural exaltation' (Diary 8). Her mental rehearsals, like 'A's' transcribing, allow her to repeat the thrill even without the presence of Johannes. But then, she never needed Johannes himself – and this is the betrayal, the source of her guilt: 'She feels him aesthetically only.' The 'aesthetic' is a function of form, not the particular person, and is therefore repeatable, endlessly transforming mere bodies into signs of desire, into reflection. Johannes's triumph is that she treats him as his diary treated her, imagining she seduces and betrays him while she merely repeats him.

The narrator describes Johannes's aesthetic transformations and repetitions in similar terms. Despite the apparent tedium of Johannes's life, Johannes discovered 'the interesting in life' and 'constantly reproduced what he has experienced in a more or less poetical manner' (Diary 3). In one whose life contains a poverty of observable events, the 'interesting' can exist only in the perpetual and simultaneous translation of experience into diary. 'A' describes

Johannes's imagination as 'not poor enough to distinguish poetry and reality from each other' (Diary 3). Because his reality is 'poetical,' it is readily retrieved as 'poetic reflection' for a 'second enjoyment.' As 'A' conceives of it, what is interesting for Johannes arises from the intertwined forms of seduction and the poetic, which enables him to extend his own experiences to other consciousnesses through repetition and elaboration. 'Reality,' and consequently his consciousness of himself as a subject, depends on the constitutive power of his langauge, the unarticulated remaining limited to the irreality of 'that nebulous realm.' It is not surprising then that once he has introduced the gaping depths of 'many-tongued reflection' with their terrifying excitement to Cordelia and 'A,' they should imitate Johannes's plan to perpetuate their readings of the story. For them also, a world that has not been transformed by narrative is unreal: they have been cast out from the Edenic garden of a natural, immediate experience of life. Consequently they must attempt to appropriate what has threatened to destroy them.

When 'A' speaks of the narrative in his preface, he displaces the interest of the text from the seduction to his own experience of reading. Speaking of the effect Cordelia's passion has had on her, he says, 'Terrible is this for her, but it will be even more terrible for him; this I can infer from my own reaction, since even I am scarcely able to control the anxiety that seizes me every time I think about the matter' (Diary 9). Cordelia was led to her state by her desire for Johannes, 'A' by his desire for the text. I have already noted that the danger and excitement were evoked by simply recopying the text, but even to think about it prompts a powerful response, much as Cordelia's thought led to 'an unnatural exaltation.' The acts of reading, transcribing and interpreting become intensely eroticized for 'A,' who serves as a model for subsequent readings of the diary. The implication is that any reader who would understand the diary must, like 'A,' invest himself in the text to know it. He must read like Cordelia who listens 'with an indescribable dread, mysterious, yet blissful . . . to the music I myself evoked and yet did not evoke' (Diary 9). 'A's' preface, that is, offers the reader a narrative that he can possess by imitating 'A's' reading: he must overstep the boundaries between reader and writer, revising for his own use what is proper to the writer.

Johannes, cunning seducer, deliberately feigns secrecy as an element of seduction, as I note above. 'A' literally repeats that ploy: Johannes 'has spread the deepest secrecy over everything, and yet there is an even deeper secret, the secret, namely, that I am in the know and that this has happened in a culpable manner' (Diary 9). Getting knowledge leads to guilt, for in order to probe the secret of another, the boundaries between the knower and his object must be crossed, the difference of otherness violated. Each of the characters confounds the distinctions between self and beloved, reader and text, and this loss of distinction leads them to a state comprising bliss and dread, the two poles of loss. Desiring to possess the secret, each finds himself part of the secret where he transforms the language of authority into the dissembling 'aesthetic' language of secrecy and seduction.

'A' says of secrecy even as he adds to it, 'There is nothing which involves so much leading astray and which is so subject to anathema as a secret.' To sin and to curse sin fall together in a breath. The confessor listening to the undecipherable turns of transgression follows the speaker into the labyrinth of endless detours. He is led into the coils of interpretation, not by a sheer innocence but, as 'A's' reading demonstrates, by a desire to enter the field and conquer the many-tongued dissembler, to establish himself as master of the secret. And there he finds only the necessities of seduction and confession, of the 'paradigm' in which 'what looks like an exit turns out to be a new entrance' (Diary 7). The good Victor Ermita's subsequent discovery and publication of 'A's' papers only confirm the efficacy of the form.

Confession and revenge

> There is nothing which involves so much leading astray and which is so
> subject to anathema as a secret.   *Diary of a Seducer*

The plot of Henry James's 'The Figure in the Carpet' centers on the 'critic's' (as I shall call the narrator) preoccupation with the mystery of the 'passion of passions' that governs all of the famous novelist Vereker's writing. He has always liked Vereker's novels, but when his editor Corvick, and later even Vereker himself, suggests that there is something more to the novels than he had noted, his appreciation becomes an obsession. His failure to discover *the* solution to Vereker's work becomes more tormenting when Corvick claims to have found it, apparently confirming its doubtful existence. Yet it seems clear enough that the critic chases a phantom.

The scorn with which the best of the story's readers tend to view the benighted critic does not, however, discourage their own critical attempts to clarify the notion of the figure. Wolfgang Iser, with a fine sense of the futility, almost immorality, of finding a 'meaning' for the figure, concludes that 'the formulated text, as Vereker and Corvick understand it, represents a pattern, a structured indicator to guide the imagination of the reader; and so the meaning can only be grasped as an image. The image provides the filling for what the textual pattern structures but leaves out' (Iser 9). Corvick and Vereker, Iser thinks, *understand* – nothing solid, of course, but they have an 'image.' And Iser shares this understanding. He joins Corvick and the great Vereker (and James too, we must say) in having a laugh at the critic. The advantage of the 'image' as a way of talking about meaning is that it remains unpresentable in language while still providing a meaning, an object for thought. Iser proposes this reading because he sees the story as being about a kind of criticism whose day has passed, that of parasites drawing truths from the artists' obscure representations, of the critics who prey on Verekers. But for all he says of Vereker, he says little of James's text except that it leads us to read against the grain of the critic: he speaks of James's story not in terms of its image but of the lesson of the master. Vereker's novels may be a structured indicator of some missing essence, but James's story, it seems, tells us something we can understand clearly.

Within the literary society of the tale, Vereker commands a position of great authority, an envied, powerful man. He is, apparently, an elusive, difficult novelist, capable of making the name of any critic who could 'get at him.' Our critic is particularly eager to achieve this goal: young, barely known and barely paid, and envious of his friend and superior Corvick, he sees Vereker as his big chance. Consequently, when Vereker himself oversteps the hermetic boundaries of the author and offers some critical commentary on his own work, the critic grasps eagerly at the threads of meaning. Yet Vereker's explanation fails to offer anything solid for the literal-minded critic to hold. '*You* miss it,' he teases, leaving the critic looking for a referent for the 'it' (FC 141). 'By my little point I mean – what shall I call it? – the particular thing I've written my books most *for*.' But Vereker does more than simply avoid making any definite statement. When the critic suggests that 'it' is 'a kind of esoteric message,' Vereker responds, 'Ah my dear fellow, it can't be described in cheap

40

journalese' (FC 143). He undermines the very language that the critic might use to understand. The effect is to leave the critic not just mystified, but impotent. It is as if he has been chastised for reaching too far and as a consequence is denied even the means to redeem his ignorance.

James's critics find themselves in a similar dilemma. James, for example, seems to speak through Vereker, asking, 'Isn't there for every writer a particular thing of that sort?' (FC 141): aren't we, that is, to take James's tale as also containing an elusive figure? Iser, to stay with one reader, understandably thinks so, and he looks to the one place in the story not mediated by the narrator for evidence: the title. Here James gives the 'key': 'Meaning is imagistic in character' (Iser 8). Perhaps it is, but we know no more about the meaning of the key by replacing 'figure' with 'image' than we would by replacing 'The very passion of his passion' with 'love' or some other ideality. For by doing so, we forgo the discourse of critical understanding and produce our own mysteries, and usually inferior ones at that. Corvick claims Vereker took him in his arms when he discovered the figure: James provides no such embrace.

But perhaps the problem lies in the notion of understanding, of mastering a mystery. If we go along with the idea that the story is itself a version of a Vereker figure, we are faced with the fact that the critic in his self-confessed obtuseness has narrated this tale and therefore, without understanding, has reproduced the figure. That is, the figure is produced not necessarily by one who understands, but by one who interprets: it is an effect of the desire to understand, not the achievement of that understanding. Consequently, while the plot of the story follows the critic's vain attempts to reveal the figure, the language of his attempts continues to reproduce its 'exquisite scheme.' The impulse to mastery, it seems, transgresses the boundaries of possible, or perhaps even proper, knowledge. It places the critic in a position of anxiety and obligation that leads him to seek release in confessing his inadequacy to another. The critic's failure is the figure's success.

The effect of the figure recurs several times throughout the story. The relationship of Vereker to the critic, for example, is doubled by the subplot of Corvick's wooing of novelist Gwendolen Erme. Corvick is ostensibly hampered in his suit by the refusal of Gwendolen's mother to die. But there is also a certain coolness on Gwendolen's part: she's too cool, at least, to marry and risk losing her mother's money. When the critic has begun to despair of ever discovering the figure, he tells Corvick of it, and Corvick immediately employs the tale to intrigue Gwendolen, evoking her 'ardent response' (FC 149). As the critic enviously notes, the two appropriate the mystery, following 'the chase for which I myself had sounded the horn' (FC 150). The critic hears from Vereker that Corvick's and Gwendolen's being engaged 'may help them' in their search, but he draws from this clue only the spiteful observation that, 'They would scarce have got so wound up, I think, if they hadn't been so in love: poor Vereker's inner meaning gave them endless occasion to put and to keep their young heads together' (FC 151). He assumes that the chase had provided an excuse for these occasions of intimacy. But being engaged is, when properly conducted, a state of deferred desire. Vereker's suggestion seems to be that the figure and such desire are linked, an idea supported by the fact that before the introduction of this mystery, their relationship had been more intellectual than passionate, certainly nothing to compare with the intimacy implied in putting young heads together. 'She wasn't pretty but was awfully interesting,' is all the critic can say in appreciation of Corvick and Gwendolen's affair (FC 135). The heightened intensity of the lovers' affection suggests that the search for the figure has provided them with a form for passion that their previous chaste lives had not.

The lovers' joint pursuit of Vereker runs across one methodological difference: Corvick wants to 'run him to earth' (FC 152) through his writing, while Gwendolen wants to meet and 'trap' him. '"But she must play fair – she *shan't* see him!"' he tells the critic. And then fearing this protest might be taken the 'wrong way' – as if Gwendolen could be interested in another man – he adds, 'She's quite incredibly literary, you know – quite fantastically.' Corvick's fear seems less unreasonable, however, a few lines later when the critic admits that he 'had taken to the man still more than [he] had ever taken to the books' (FC 152). If the critic could be so seduced, Miss Erme might, too. The mystery that had first drawn Corvick's and Gwendolen's young heads together now threatens to lead the maiden's elsewhere. This possibility helps explain Corvick's desire to run Vereker to earth on his own terms: he wants to master the figure and thus become 'the man.' He fails, however, and frustrated in love and criticism, Corvick decides to take a foreign assignment. He tells the critic that his engagement with Gwendolen is off, at which the critic, in a display of narcissism, suspects (and denies) that he may be the cause of an estrangement: 'Well, if he had taken the turn of jealousy, for instance, it could scarcely be jealousy of me' (FC 154). Jealousy it may be, but the more likely object is Vereker.

Corvick subsequently announces from India that he has discovered the figure, but he tells Gwendolen that she must marry him before he will disclose the secret to her. She grants her immediate assent, despite her mother's lingering health. When she tells her news to the critic, she says that of course they were always engaged, and moreover promises that, under the circumstances, her mother *must* agree to a prompt death. This radical alteration in circumstances results, it appears, solely from Corvick's knowing the secret, not from his actually making any disclosures about it. Once he has begun writing the 'last word' on Vereker (writing him off), Gwendolen is eager not only to marry quickly but even, apparently, to hurry her mother underground.

The critic speculates vaguely about Gwendolen, particularly about the circumstances of her mother's death (Why *had* she succumbed so promptly?) feeling, curiously, like a 'coerced spectator' (FC 162) to the affair. Somewhere in her plotting, he is certain, is the solution to Vereker's mystery. And yet there is no indication throughout these events that Gwendolen has fallen in love in any conventional sense, even though her desires have been aroused to new heights. She marries and honeymoons, and her new husband straightaway falls on his head and dies before revealing the secret in an essay. The personal tragedies of the two deaths pass quickly, however, leaving the critic to wonder: 'Had she seen the idol unveiled? Had there been a private ceremony for a palpitating audience of one? For what else but that had the nuptials taken place?'' (FC 163). Everything indicates that Gwendolen actually did marry just to hear the secret, even to the extent that her possession of it did actually serve as 'a counterpoise to her grief' (FC 163) over Corvick's and her mother's deaths, and this fascinates the critic.

In fact, the idea that Gwendolen may now possess the secret of the figure is enough to make the critic into a suitor, though not one who could face the prospect of actually marrying to see the idol. His suspicion that she is Corvick's, and Vereker's, heir seems confirmed by the interest she inspires in the 'literary circles referred to in the papers' and, particularly, in the reviewer Drayton Deane. Although she was an unknown novelist, reviewed only by her fiancé until his death, her novels suddenly take on a new power: 'I don't review . . . I'm reviewed' (FC 167), she tells the critic when he suggests she review Vereker's last book. Everything she does indicates that she is one who knows, and it makes her, after Vereker's death, the sole master of the critic's desire.

What emerges from this paraphrase of a plot is not a definition of the figure but a pattern of effects that arise from the desire to know about the figure. More specifically, each character who knows about the figure (not necessarily what it means) uses this knowledge to evoke a response from someone who stands in a relation of rivalry or opposition to him. When a character hears the story of the figure, he responds either by attempting to possess the bearer of the secret or by meticulously retracing the works of its formulator in an attempt to surpass or appropriate him, to 'get *at* him.' Each works under the assumption that the figure can be discovered and articulated, even though each of its literary manifestations – Vereker's works, Corvick's manuscript, and Gwendolen's *Overmastered* – fails to reveal it. Yet something is passed from one character to another, the critic's account of which is yet another vessel of the figure. The figure propagates itself without the enlightenment of those touched by it.

In the first interview the critic has with Vereker, Vereker mentions the figure, claiming it has an evident and concrete presence, 'as concrete there as a bird in a cage, a bait on a hook, a piece of cheese in a mousetrap' (FC 144). The images Vereker chooses here are figures of entrapment. The critic takes up the bait of the concrete, suggesting it may be '"in the language. Perhaps a preference for the letter P: . . . Papa, potatoes, prunes – that sort of thing?" Vereker [was] suitably indulgent: he only said I hadn't got the right letter' (FC 144). The hint seems almost too broad, especially when we know that 'it dots every i.' And when on the next page Corvick, excited by what he thinks is the hiddenness of the figure, says 'there was more in Vereker than met the eye,' the critic responds that 'the eye seemed what the printed page had been expressly invented to meet' (FC 145). So superficial a reading understandably irritates the profound Corvick, but the pun on 'eye' is obvious.

The figures of the 'I' and the trap suggest an allegory at work in the interview scene. The critic, eager for Vereker's praise, had been unintentionally rebuffed and unsettled by Vereker at a dinner party. In an attempt to flatter Vereker, their hostess had given him the critic's review, which Vereker judged 'all right – the usual twaddle' (FC 139). Vereker, discovering the insulted reviewer was present, catches him late at night and draws him into an intimate conversation. Both the critic's review and Vereker's novel fade before the fact of the personal attention and passion of the great man: 'The hour, the place, the unexpectedness deepened the impression: he couldn't have done anything more intensely effective' (FC 140). The critic, of course, assumes the circumstances were accidental, but as Vereker's conversation makes clear, he is an artist in his smallest gesture. He teases the critic's interest, tantalizing him with his strange metaphors and moments of seeming confidence, until the thoroughly taken critic exclaims, 'You fire me as I've never been fired' (EC 143). But for all they say, when Vereker departs, the critic remains unsatisfied, standing by his bedroom door as he 'looked after [Vereker] rather yearningly.' The object of desire leaves, advising him to 'give it up,' the sort of advice that inevitably draws the opposite response: 'If I had had one of his books at hand I'd have repeated my recent act of faith – I'd have spent half the night with him' (FC 145).

The situation, for all its literary demeanor, employs the form and language of a seduction. After having displayed the critic's inadequacy as a reader to him, Vereker seems to offer himself, the 'I,' as the lure into the trap, the compensation for the critic's sense of personal affront. The man himself sits there – 'I can see him still, on my rug' – guarantor of a truth (life, passion) behind the inscrutable text. But 'the man' withdraws. That appealing self is not really his to bestow since by his own testimony it is nothing but the figure manifested in every word he writes. The writer has already found that the penalty for writing is to discover that he has no expressible self to produce: like Satan, he finds that no self-creation is possible, only the creation of an 'I.' And it is this 'I' that tempts the critic to seek a truth beyond the text, beyond even the body of the man Vereker himself. As it was for Vereker, the critic's attempt at knowledge produces a sense of longing and obligation for which no direct satisfaction exists. Vereker seduces the critic with the 'I' and binds him to an oblique path back through all of his novels to try ultimately to possess the texts' life.

The Corvick–Gwendolen love plot, then, is less a subplot than an extension in overtly sexual terms of an allegory initiated by Vereker's confession, love in their case being little more than an effect produced by the pursuit of the suddenly 'lost' figure. The discursive, explanatory aspects of the narrative appeal to the 'subtle' minds of critics, while the confessional aspects operate continuously in a non-representational, allegorical mode. The figure, the illusory 'I,' exists only as the allegorization of itself, always present to the eye, yet resistant to interpretation or possession.

The peculiar power the narrative of the figure has depends on the way the 'literary circles' read, the critic being the exemplar of the crowd. *The Middle*, the pointedly entitled journal he and Corvick write for, defines their position of mediation, forever between the authorial voice and the reader's full appreciation of the word. (The critic's explanation of the title, that the journal appears in the middle of the week, is sensible.) The narrative opens with the critic's resentment – too few pence earned, fewer certainly than Corvick – and in the delight he feels in having a chance to appropriate Vereker's reputation to advance his own. Each critic, in fact, has as his ultimate intention the appropriation of the one he writes about. Corvick, for instance, had been 'really splendid' in reviewing 19-year-old Gwendolen's first bad novel, producing a review superior to the work. And he desires, as I've mentioned, the 'last word' on Vereker, after which even Vereker, presumably, would have nothing to say. Even illiterate Lady Jane takes part. She claims the critic's review expresses 'what *I* always felt' (FC 138), as if the reviewer had somehow plumbed her own emotional depths and merely copied them; and she literally writes over the review: 'Just see there, and there, where I've dashed it, how he brings it out.' Each of them feels the priority of another's text and writes specifically in order to supplant it. The 'I' of that earlier text seems to deny each his own autonomy. The 'original' must be simply an excuse for each one's own writing, even if writing only copies the prior text, 'to trace the figure in the carpet through every convolution, to reproduce it in every tint' (FC 161).

Vereker plays on this resentment in 'literary circles.' When the critic asks Vereker to 'initiate him into the mystery,' the writer takes this desire and sets it to work: the figure is ' "naturally the thing for the critic to look for. It strikes me," my visitor added, smiling, "even as the thing for the critic to find" ' (FC 142). Vereker assigns the critic's task: he is both to look for the 'little trick' and to 'initiate' others into the sanctum of Vereker's work. He can make the critic into his servant, his propagator, because 'the critic just isn't a plain man: if he were, pray, what would he be doing in his neighbor's garden?' (FC 145). The critic is a kind of thief whom the wily Vereker employs to harvest his crop. A critic's desire to appropriate the labor of another is the force the writer inverts to ensure the perpetuation of his work.

As a critic the narrator finds himself confined to rigid forms, to the community of the literary circle, to 'journalese,' as Vereker calls it; he desires the openness of life and passion, the triumph of his individual talent, a poetic voice. Similarly, although Corvick must obey the dictates of money – waiting for Gwendolen's inheritance, making a 'plausible arrangement with the usual big fat publisher' – he wants the love of Gwendolen and Vereker. Both men are bound by conventions while they desire transcendence. Vereker's work seems to authorize such desires by realizing what the critics only imagine. Consequently they imagine a magnificent, confessing 'I' speaking through every line of Vereker's work, 'the man' behind the work. And yet 'cleverness' is all they can wrest from Vereker in their own prose. Vereker's language will not yield to a sudden clarification that the critic seeks, for the 'idol' is entirely in its verbal surface.

This 'surface' is an allegory in Paul de Man's sense of the word, a spatializing of temporal development in a text (Man 207). By contrast with the allegory, the symbol proposes to bridge the gap between subjective and objective worlds. Symbols claim a correspondence with a larger totality of transcendent truths. They resemble the pre-Saussurean sign, that conjunction of word and meaning in a unity. The problem this concept presents for de Man, as it did for Saussure, is that the signified takes on a mystical, ineffable autonomy, becomes an image, to recall Iser's term, divorced from language. Whether or not such totalizing gestalts inhabit the minds of readers, such meanings are by their nature beyond the writer's, or critic's, capacity for representation. Yet, as we have seen in this story, something is transmitted from character to character.

Allegory, however, is semiotic: its meaning does not reside in a referent, but in the relations between signs. This relationship is on the page, but it does not exclude a sense of temporal order. De Man explains it this way: 'this relationship between signs necessarily contains a constitutive temporal element; it remains necessary, if there is to be allegory, that the allegorical sign refer to another sign that precedes it. The meaning constituted by the allegorical sign can then consist only in the *repetition* (in the Kierkegaardian sense of the term) of a previous sign with which it can never coincide, since it is of the essence of this previous sign to be pure anteriority' (Man 207). The Kierkegaardian sense of repetition develops from the emptiness of any one event. Repetition is structural rather than essential, always recalling an earlier relation between signifiers, not the meaning of the prior sign. Consequently, the allegorical repetition does not move toward an identity of a text and its truth, steadily reenforcing the correspondence of the allegory to the original situation. Instead, each repetition reveals the inadequacy of the previous narrative to reveal its own meaning. The apparent attempt of an allegory to retell a story more clearly, to explain what remains indeterminate, looks back to that failed narrative to justify its own project. But at the same time that earlier narrative remains inexplicable, the 'pure anteriority' it can never match.

This is not the traditional allegory which is sustained by a parallel true text: imagine, for example, that Gwendolen's novels get better because she does in fact find the right letter, 'P' or 'I.' Rather, the allegory, though shaped at every turn by that 'anteriority,' can never attain its illusory truth, and thus can have no conclusion where reality and allegory meet. In 'The Figure in the Carpet' any approach to a solution to the mystery is followed by evasion. The elaborately digressive Jamesian subordination, the frequent indeterminate pronouns, the seemingly familiar plots (mystery, love), and, most effectively, the sheer perversity of the narrative voice (the critic with his ingenious false leads and pompous stupidity) – all these devices conspire to suggest and defeat answers. And each reader or critic in the story, hoping to reconcile the demands of form and passion, of popular acclaim and individuality, or of money and love, pursues Vereker's texts in the hope of appropriating the authorial 'I' that they hope stands behind, anterior to every text.

The critic is the proper choice to hear Vereker's confession, both because he is so intensely driven by the desires and resentment, and because he writes and can therefore be counted on to perpetuate the figure through subsequent victims. He recounts Vereker's story in order to share his sense of loss and desire with others. Corvick is consumed by curiosity, believing as the critic does that he might discover the solution; Gwendolen is no less convinced that a solution exists and can be articulated, and she is, consequently, 'chilled by my apparent indisposition to oblige them with the detail of what Vereker had said to me' (FC 150). The critic's own failure governs his retelling, ensuring that others will follow out his own path. Looking back, he attempts to master Vereker, while he also turns to his listeners, tantalizing them with an object he can present only as missing.

The critic's position is not necessarily, however, perpetually unconscious servitude to Vereker. When Gwendolen dies, he goes to her widowed husband, Drayton Deane, assuming that his nuptials must also have involved an unveiling of the idol. Deane had never heard of the figure, but as the critic tells him of it he begins to resemble his rival: 'I may say that to-day as victims of unappeased desire there isn't a pin to choose between us. The poor man's state is almost my consolation; there are really moments when I feel it to be quite my revenge' (FC 173). He has learned to do to others what Vereker has done to him. More significantly, he has reshaped Deane's desires so that Deane is now an imitation of himself, an allegory of his own 'I.' This is Vereker's power and his revenge: to transform his reader's narrative's into allegories of himself, but of a self that never exists except as a prior narrative. The critic has learned his lesson so well that one could say he dotted every 'I' in the story.

The narrators I have discussed – Augustine (the narrator, not necessarily the sainted father), Johannes, and the critic – all share a sense of exclusion from an order that is more or less accepted by their societies, a sense which denies them an easy place within that society. Each addresses a relatively conventional reader within a discourse that undermines the reader's conventions while it generates its own ordering activity. James's 'critic' finds that his meeting with Vereker has deprived him of the pleasant sense that he can get at the writers he writes about. Having searched in the Author's garden for a tempting knowledge, he has found himself knowing nothing but loss. Without being quite conscious of what he is doing, he finds himself infecting others with his sense of loss and his agonizing desire to know even more. For each of Vereker's victims, reading ceases to be a happy gathering of chestnuts and becomes rather a life-consuming, and life-giving, pursuit. Only at the end does the critic discover, still perhaps just half-consciously, that his bitter failure has been transformed to his only joy, his 'passion of passions.'

Augustine is too rigorous a thinker to accept any concept of God that implies one can fully understand Him. Those who attempt to understand God through the Bible are reading incorrectly, idolatrously. Augustine pursues his own salvation (and insists his readers can train themselves to do the same) through a perpetual rethinking of the wayward paths toward God. To retrace one's sins in confession becomes the model for salvation.

And Johannes, finding himself surrounded by people eager to fall in love, offers them the language of passion, a promise of satisfaction for any willing to betray the boundaries of normal life. But then he mocks those who desire a total union of hearts by showing such unions to be half a trick of speech and half (the poorer half) a trick of the body. That trick of speech, however, leads to the 'many-tongued,' 'nebulous realm,' a realm more attractive than love itself. His readers, Cordelia and the editor 'A,' having been deprived of love's delusions through their own transgressions, submit themselves to the discourse they have learned from him because it fills them with excitement, pleasure, and desire: it returns them to a world almost as melting as that of love, but located in the repetition of a confession rather than in the idol love.

I emphasize these parallels to make clear the activity I call confession: one who has transgressed tells his story, which draws the reader into another sort of transgression for pleasure, for power, but a transgression followed also out of obligation. The narrator finds confirmation and consolation for his loss in the others' imitation, while the reader's pain of imitating becomes, in time, the pleasure of usurpation and revenge. The readers become the writers, the seduced the seducers: interest in sin inevitably becomes involvement. It is always this relation of the confessor to his listener that I am exploring, working through the form of authority – sexual, theological, critical – exploited by the confessor. As examples, the particular forms of authority in these three texts are less important than the confessional forms they work within. They reveal confession to be a dynamic that can emerge in any discourse addressed to another when the accepted, conventional languages of truth are disrupted. At that point of disruption, the motives of communication and representation are supplanted by the desire to dominate the discourse of others. The

50

writers' intentions may be virtuous or evil, their motives may be conscious or unconscious, but within each text run forces of desire and obligation that touch the deepest, most anxious hopes of their readers.

3

The embroidered sin:
confessional evasion in *The Scarlet Letter*

I

After having agreed with Hester to abandon Boston for Europe,
Dimmesdale returns to the city in an exaltation of guilt and writes
his final election day sermon with unprecedented fluency and power.
He 'fancied himself inspired,' but is surprised 'that Heaven should
see fit to transmit the grand and solemn music of its oracles through
so foul an organ-pipe as he' (SL 29). He cannot resolve the paradox
created by the metaphor he has chosen to express the relation of the
minister of the Word to The Word. The 'organ-pipe' implies that he
is merely a conduit for the spirit God breathes through him, giving
this breath sensible form without altering its meaning. The clarity of
Dimmesdale's transmission would seem to depend on the minister's
self-effacing purity, on the absence of the eccentric, supplementary
voice of an unrepentant sinner. Yet this sermon, like all Dimmesdale's most effective sermons, follows his most flagrant
hypocrisies, a juxtaposition he sees as an astonishing coincidence
without suspecting that his duplicity may in fact be the source of his
power.

The metaphor of the 'foul organ-pipe' suggests the minister's
belief that sin should impair his fitness to translate spirit into speech
and leave him speaking a fallen, earthly tongue: sin should sever
language from truth. This is consistent with Puritan conventions of
interpretation: as Bercovitch describes it, the proper reader and
writer must efface his subjective individuality in an imitation of
Christ: 'To speak plainly was not to speak simply, and not at all to
speak artlessly. It meant speaking the Word – making language
itself, as self-expression, an *imitatio Christi* because it conformed to
scripture' (*Puritan Origins* 29). God's immanence in the words of the
Bible implied that, by imitating the Bible's style, one could speak
God's truth. But the Puritans always recognized the necessity of the
exegete, 'who brings spirit to fact and carries the light of meaning in
himself' (*Puritan Origins* 112), and the dangers or error if the spirit is

lacking. One of the strictures laid down for exegesis was that spirit be present: 'Hermeneutics presupposes a reader transformed in the image of the spirit he sets out to discover' (*Puritan Origins* 111). Only the elect, those clean of obscuring intrusions of a self, should be able to read the true significations in the signs. Dimmesdale has chosen a course that has opened a gap between himself and God, and hence, he supposes, between his word and The Word, and yet astonishingly to him, his language is unimpaired. The very act of transgression in the forest, the hypocritical repetition of the sin that should have led to the death of the Word, becomes on the contrary the origin of new vitality. The movement of the whole book reinforces this point: the source of Dimmesdale's 'Tongue of Flame' is his sin.

This opening does not merely show that Dimmesdale, mystified by his dwelling within Puritan theology, cannot understand his own rhetorical power, though that is true enough. Rather, it shows, ironically, that he achieves his greatest spiritual success by using the forms of Puritan orthodoxy to express a secular, sexual passion. A psychological interpretation could readily explain the transfer of passion in terms of libidinal displacement (Crews 105), but that would not explain the particular formal power of his sermon to fill his listeners with so great a religious ecstasy. In *The American Jeremiad* (the title refers to political–religious speeches, like Dimmesdale's election day sermon), Bercovitch argues that the Puritan ideology – and, to some extent, all subsequent American ideology – was formed by a rhetoric that blended historical and prophetic modes, the secular with the sacred. The Jeremiad accustomed Puritans to seeing every event as expressing in its particularity a divine intention (*Jeremiad* 9 & 15). By arrogating the language of the divine to his individual experience, Dimmesdale can display his sin and shame while remaining certain that the dirty effusions of his organ will go unheard, despite any intentions he may have to confess truly.

The capacity of the confessional mode to turn to deception in Dimmesdale's mouth derives from a doubleness in Puritan theology. The Puritans applied a Catholic tradition of typological interpretation to their own experience, seeing America as an embodiment of Biblical 'types.' But as Feidelson points out, they did so 'gingerly,' always attempting to restrict the 'multiple meanings inherent in real things' (Feidelson 89) to a single meaning. Any attempt to capture 'the whole of reality in the texture of a rational language' (94) was

condemned to failure by the requirements of each individual to interpret a word and world that do not behave rationally.[1] Puritanism
depended on a continuous reinterpretation of the world and men to
determine God's will; consequently, antinomianism, the voice of
renegade individualism, posed a constant danger to the coherence of
the church. As Milton's struggles reveal, personal faith and individual will resemble each other too nearly for one to distinguish
between them with a comfortable certainty. William K. Stoever links
the two, identifying Puritanism with the dialectic of covenant
theology and antinomianism, 'newness and order,' nature and grace:
'The individual Puritan's life, like his divinity, moved back and forth
between personal experience of gracious transformation and obe-
dience to the order dictated by God's sovereign will' (Stoever 18).
Both alternatives require an interpretation of signs, internal or scrip-
tural, to determine what is lawful. It is difficult, perhaps impossible,
for those involved in sin to recognize it as sin with certainty. I am
not referring here to the simple violation of an expressly stated law
– a legal adultery, theft or lie – for sin per se is a violation of a
transcendent law, and such laws are famous for their ambiguity, both
in statement and authority. Before the act (and sometimes after), sin
is a matter for speculation – if Lucifer had turned out to be a god,
his rebellion would have been no sin – and only the dismal consequences can confirm his error. Although those who stand firmly
within the norms may judge clearly, the difference between reason
and will is never clear to the one contemplating his desire. The
danger is always that in the attempt to obey God's 'sovereign will,'
one must trust to the notoriously unreliable inner promptings of
spirit.[2] And if Dimmesdale cannot distinguish inspiration from will,
how should his listeners? There would be no reason to suspect the
passions aroused in them by Dimmesdale's speech might be a
response not to Dimmesdale's faith, but to his own private passion.

If there seemed any sin to detect in Dimmesdale's sermons, the
listener would have more reason to think it was his own, not the
minister's. Believing themselves innately depraved and saved only by
election, Puritans could know their state of grace only through the
signs of election. As Michael Colacurcio points out, it is less one's
good actions than one's response to sin that provides these signs
(490). Sin is, it appears, an ironic necessity to any knowledge of
oneself or God. Dimmesdale would also be subject to this necessity.

Without attributing any conscious intention to him, it seems clear that his choice of Hester is partly a function of his desire to transgress – which of the white-bosomed virgins of Boston couldn't he legitimately have married if he had wished? D. H. Lawrence with the genius of his *idée fixe* sees that the 'chief charm' of their adultery lay in its being wrong (111–12). But what Lawrence cannot see is that it is precisely in being 'wrong' that adultery has meaning.

It is unfortunate for religions that few acts identified as sins produce the immediate punishment that would confirm their offensiveness to God. The most dismal natural consequence of Dimmesdale's attempt is Hester's pregnancy, an occasion the church must bless even while condemning the cause. The community does, however, have the means to judge and punish in God's place, though the community does not have quite God's prescience: Dimmesdale's sin could produce the knowledge of an 'affirmed world'[3] only if it were publicly confessed.[4] His pulpit confessions, however, only arouse adoration in his listeners, confusing rather than clarifying the structure of God's order. Dimmesdale's famous capacity to 'express the highest truths through the humblest medium of familiar words and images' (SL 104) seems to be less a matter of granting his listeners an insight into obscure realms of knowledge than of allowing them to substitute what they know about their common world for what they wish to know about heaven. The parishioners' radical misreading of Dimmesdale's sermons is possible only because sin, like God, is perceived as a mystery: and Dimmesdale, unwilling himself to understand his motives, finds it only too easy to produce his own mystery by introducing uninterpretable elements into his confession. It is impossible for the parishioners, sensing the mystery, to tell whether it represents the hidden divinity, or the subtle evasions of the liar. That is, for those who live within the dualism of salvation and damnation, there is something strangely interchangeable about saints and sinners.

This collapse of the difference between saint and sinner is probably less a matter of intention (hypocritical or spiritual) on the saint/sinner's part than of an identity between their modes of discourse. Such a conclusion is suggested if we reason, like Nietzsche, back from effect rather than forward from intent. The effect Dimmesdale has on people is described in detail:

The people knew not the power that moved them thus. They deemed the young clergyman a miracle of holiness. They fancied him the mouthpiece of Heaven's messages of wisdom, and rebuke, and love. In their eyes the very ground on which he trod was sanctified. The virgins of the church grew pale around him, victims of a passion so imbued with religious sentiment that they imagined it to be all religion, and brought it openly, in their white bosoms, as their most acceptable sacrifice before the altar.   (SL 104–5)

Most striking in this passage is the tremendous power Dimmesdale has over both the emotions and intellects of his listeners. They 'know not the power that moved them,' but in their wise innocence they imagine that the abyss in understanding Dimmesdale opens represents the depths of their unfathomable god. The gap between the spoken word and an immediate intuition of the divine could be represented exactly by the gaping duplicities of the hypocrite's word. In both cases, elaborate failings of Dimmesdale's language to embody truth (whether secular or divine) give him power. As John Franzosa has written of the 'inflationary' language of 'Rappaccini's Daughter,' when the values that support a language are undermined, the reader will attempt to 'fill out [the writer's] incomplete and elusive self-representation' and confer authority on him, making him 'an object of idolatry' (15 & 22n). In other words, Dimmesdale, minister or hypocrite, has the highly flattering experience of being taken for a god.

II

Like Hester's letter, which encloses her 'in a sphere by herself' (SL 44), the minister's confessions set him apart from the community without fulfilling their 'office' of producing a repentant sinner. His rhetorical elaborations before the congregation resemble the 'fantastically embroidered' 'A' Hester wears: in both cases the richness of the embellishment does not clarify the sin, but, like Derrida's 'supplement,' they add something that threatens to replace the sin, transforming the transparent mark of sin into something strangely familiar.[5] The effect of Dimmesdale's confessional evasions is his continued need to confess and do penance: 'Of penance, I have had enough! Of penitence, there has been none!' (SL 138). Penance should lead to repentance, and if it does not, then it does not purge sin but adds to it, providing ever new occasions for confession. Hester and Dimmesdale both indulge in tasks of 'penance' with an ardor suggestive of their illegitimate embrace. His employment of a 'bloody scourge' in the fashion of Catholics does not chasten his flesh (the ritual appears not to have its proper result on a non-Catholic) but merely draws his attention to his body in guilty pleasure; and fasting make his knees shake, mimicking the palsy of passion (SL 105). The repressed erotic elements of his scourging and trembling fast become explicit in the scaffold scene during his fantasies of detection (the blushing man trembling in the red dawn light while 'young virgins' rush with 'scantly' covered 'white bosoms' to see him) and the two 'thrillings' of his heart at the sound of Pearl's laugh and her touch: 'there came what seemed a tumultuous rush of new life . . . pouring like a torrent into his heart and hurrying through all his veins' (SL 111). Dimmesdale's penance effectively functions as a repetition of the sin he would transcend.[6]

This power of confession and penance to transform an apparently clear transgression into an ambiguity woven into the fabric of the community is displayed by Hester, the 'living sermon.' The legal penalty for adultery (though one not always exacted) in Hester's Boston is death (Sl 50), but something in Hester's situation arouses the 'great mercy and tenderness of heart' of her judges and allows her to remain in the midst of the community. 'This woman is youthful and fair, and doubtless was strongly tempted to her fall,' one townsman comments. 'Doubtless,' that self-belying negation, reveals in its claim of certainty a temptation that is far from mastered. It attributes to Hester a desire that the appreciative townsman does not recognize as his own, a self-deception made possible by the absence of the object of Hester's desire. This ignorance about the father frees thought from the restrictions of a conclusive history, transforming a tale of lust into the open possibility of passion for all goodmen. Passion desires the unattainable, transcendent object, and therefore oversteps the capacity of any completed predication: its meaning is always elsewhere. Hester, lacking her mate, becomes a free sign of over-reaching desire, a sign capable of entering any construction the townspeople might provide. Hester provides an occasion for speculation and inquiry, activities that in themselves produce the desire they disguise as mercy. Considering the treatment that women received at the hands of the Puritan leaders (Hawthorne's ancestors among them), it is reasonable to think that the judges would have been less tender-hearted had the inconclusiveness of her affair not piqued their interest. The effectiveness of Hester's 'sermon' seems to depend on the mystery of her sin, because hers, like Dimmesdale's, does more to arouse excitement than revulsion. When Mr Wilson notes that the lack of a known father gives 'every good Christian man . . . a title to show a father's kindness towards the poor, deserted babe' (SL 86), he opens the implication that any man might have had the happiness of fathering the child. Hester's indeterminate state allows the entire community an involvement with a discourse of desire, transgression, and sin and a taste of the passionate experience such involvement entails without, however, their having to recognize their complicity in the sin.

Hester's sin being in the past, only the signs, both natural (the child) and artificial (the A), are visible. Simple indicators though they are, their meaning is unstable. Like the terms of Dimmesdale's sermons, they are borrowed from a conventional discourse by Hester, who then uses them for her own ends. When Hester first emerges from prison, the point which draws all attention is the A, 'fantastically embroidered and illuminated upon her bosom' (SL 44). Rather than placing her within the order of the community, the effect of the A is to enclose her 'in a sphere by herself.' It is not the letter specifically that effects this estrangement, but the oddness of the embroidery that transforms the expected letter into something unfamiliar. Hester's talent, which would be an admirable virtue in anyone else, becomes by its context something indeterminate. The good wives of Boston are not even able to decide whether the embroidery should be viewed as a brazen display of pride or a sign of penance – the youngest defends Hester saying, 'not a stitch in that embroidered letter, but she has felt it in her heart' (SL 44). In either case, Hester's continual elaboration on the A prevents either the embroiderer or the viewer from allowing the letter to disappear into the folds of custom where its danger as sin could be veiled, even forgotten. The embroidery provokes their consciences.

The letter is always new, always strange, and consequently never fully incorporated into the conventional language. With each addition Hester makes to it, diverting it from that convention, the A suggests some new meaning. This does not clarify Hester's sin. Adultery exists by virtue of the limits placed on desire. Social, legal, and religious strictures repress a polymorphous, dispersive sexuality in a community, channeling it along lines that define familial and social organization. Adultery crosses the line; but it is another matter to blur the line. In this respect, Hester's embroidery is an uncanny representation of her violation: it attaches itself to the formerly distinct letter, permanently altering the townspeople's perception of the sin. Embroidery, like trope and figure, is in Puritan theory mere adornment of the truth, and 'interpretation was a simple process of reduction' (Feidelson 85), but when the embroidery literally confuses the limits of the letter, it becomes unclear how to reduce. The letter is displaced from its role within a distinct and exiled syntax of sin and begins to invade the common speech. In its marginal interaction with the mysterious letter (its mystery deepened by Hester's concealing silence, that 'wonderous strength'), the embroidery mediates between the ineffable sin and the repressed desire of the Puritan observers.

In Hester's community the principal purpose of such luxurious needlework is ostensibly to 'give majesty to the forms in which a new government manifested itself to the people,' 'to add the richer and more spiritual adornment of human ingenuity' (SL 63). To such ends, the work done by Hester's tainted hands finds a high demand among her judges. The narrator, as usual, studiously avoids providing an explanation for Hester's vogue, addressing the puzzle with his own elaboration of possibilities. He suggests that the powerful men desire to 'mortify vanity'; that Hester's work inspires the same 'morbid curiosity that gives a fictious value even to common or worthless things' (63). Each possibility, however, indicates that the 'spiritual' value of her embroidery has been enhanced by its coincidental adornment of sin: sin has become associated with the 'spiritual.' Transgression and transcendence both suggest a realm beyond the law. And like the virgins listening to Dimmesdale's confessions who imagine their feelings to be 'all religion,' the richly adorned people, knowing their seamstress has ranged beyond the limits of law, feel themselves dressed in a more spiritual cloth.

Embroidery is a go-between for two realms of meaning: the spiritual and the sinful. The Bostonians' conscious interest in the embroidery is motivated by a desire for spirit, a goal remaining always beyond immediate knowledge. However, only the signs of spirit can ever be present, and signs necessarily suffer the dangerous passage through interpretation. The anxiety produced among a devout people by this state of uncertainty could explain the wish for a short cut that avoids the endless detour of interpretation. Sin, with its illusion of presence, seems to provide that route. Foucault writes of this alternative: 'In that zone which our culture affords for our gestures and speech, transgression provides not only the sole manner of discovering the sacred in its unmediated substance, but also a way of recomposing its empty form, its absence, through which it becomes all the more scintillating' (30). The interest in things spiritual, because they can be recognized only through sin, is increased by spirit's scandalous association with sin. Consequently, the desire to engage in the language of spirit, to 'recompose its empty form,' leads one back through confession to the exciting language of sin.

The problem with this formulation is that Hester's act of adultery is as irrecoverably absent in time as spirit is absent through transcendence. If the sin were that physical act, it still would not provide the substantial proof of transgression, despite the undeniable evidence of the resulting child. But the sin is neither in conception nor even in the contact of bodies. Sin, to be sin, requires a violation of the spirit, which lies in the couple's attempt to achieve meaning for themselves outside the signifying structures of the church. Their physical union is dangerous only as the dramatization of a spiritual union in which they unsurp meaning, for it casts doubt on the spiritual authority of the entire community. When Dimmesdale hesitates at one point, Hester reminds him that they had said their action has a 'consecration of its own' (SL 140). The phrase represses the element of physical desire, projecting it onto a metaphysical plane where the merely illegal could be sin or salvation. By signifying sexual intercourse, the child signifies the desire for an unattainable spiritual union. But the child is only one manifestation of their desire, and perhaps the least exciting to the parishioners.

All desire produces activity, and when the object is denied, desire moves along detours of displaced gratification. Hester's desire for Dimmesdale is restrained by the pressures of guilt and society from the opening moment of the book, but clearly that desire never abates. Just as Dimmesdale's penance seems only to add to his ardor, Hester's embroidery appears as a displacement of her desire. Although it is certainly a continual, painful reminder of her sin, it also reminds her of what led her to the act. Embroidery allows her to exercise her desire, literally to repeat the private act of signification that denies the hermeneutic monopoly of the church. Because the sin is not the act but the desire for the self-consecrated break with the community's sacred body, the extravagance of Hester's stitchery both represents the sin and is itself a rebellion against the strictures of the norm, a resurfacing of desire. Under normal circumstances the cultural and religious structures of the community maintain the boundaries of law, not as a matter of revealed truth but as *doxa*, as second Nature. Then adultery is safe, speakable; it is the unnatural act which remains outside the community, confined to an expelled victim. But Hester violates the convention and returns adultery to the center of the community as a disruptive desire. She finds her desire answered by the responding desires of each who looks on her, whether in sympathy or hatred. She finds a community of sin, a 'mystic sisterhood' (SL 66), and this informs her passion with a social reality.

It is not a specific sin that Hester's public confession suggests, nor is it one desire. Since the object, and hence the exact form of her desire, remains unknown, hers can serve as the 'type,' as the narrator calls it, the model and mirror of all desires in those who see her. Edgar A. Dryden gathers the various effects desires produce under the term 'enchantment.' The chief characteristic of enchantment is the illusion that difference is overcome: between the self and another, lover and beloved, writer and reader, and ultimately present and origin in a magnificent collapse. He draws a comparison between love and reading: 'For Hawthorne the fascination of reading like the fascination of love is the result of the irresistible lure exerted by another person's existence, but, unlike the relation between the beloved and the lover, that between author and reader is generated by a will to power' (107). That lure, however, is exerted not by a true 'existence,' but by the illusion of an autonomous self. The beloved, like the author, appears as the more complete being, a self-sufficient other who, if she does not already possess her desire, knows what it is she truly wants. Her power is in the promise that the difference between a mute hunger and satisfaction can be overcome. The illusion that sustains her power depends on lovers', like readers', desire for enchantment. Hester, as a model of the writer, participates in the will to power Dryden identifies, arousing the desire of others in imitation of her own. She need not be conscious of this intention. What I suggest is that she achieves the effects she does through the community's complicity. As an active principle of transgression, she invites them into an enchantment with sin, into the illusion of a divinely ordained way to heaven marked off by her straying. She takes their laws and their scarlet letter and, by violating the limits with a complacent beauty (no taint of sin), reveals the arbitrary structure of all that has defined and restricted desire. She give the A that had spoken strictly of adultery the power to speak for the community's longings that, because there was no language to speak them, had remained dumb torments.

III

It is easy to see Hester as the hero of the story here: her actions transform a community and help to free a people from repressions they had no way of addressing. Dimmesdale's motivations, however, appear to change from the relatively innocent rebellion of passion against the restraints of the law into an ugly delight in sin. At first, his adultery suggests an impulse toward transcendence to be achieved either through a communion with Hester or through an experience of divine retribution evoked by his transgression. Rebellion is a common enough reaction to a youthful suspicion that cultural conventions lack authority. But when the adultery produces neither transcendence nor punishment, he discovers that the duplicities of his habitual speech, which seem to deny him an authentic confession, evoke an eager complicity in the Puritan community. The parishioners hear the embroidered sin and abandon themselves to its author: they do not respond to him as a sinner, but as if he were a saint on earth. They desire to find in their minister the embodiment of divine authority, someone who will confirm their sense of boundaries to be violated. Like Dimmesdale in his adultery, they find in listening to him the horror and promise of transgression: they mimic his sin. What Dimmesdale discovers and (perhaps unconsciously) exploits is the pleasure of power, the narcissistic gratification of finding reflected in his listeners not the 'solemn music' of the divine but idolatry.

The power of Dimmesdale's text to involve the reader is not limited to the particulars of the narrative plot but is, rather, part of the structure of the text. But how does the narrative do this? At one point the narrator reflects on Dimmesdale's hypocrisy:

"I, your pastor, whom you so reverence and trust, am utterly a pollution and a lie!"

More than once, Mr. Dimmesdale had gone into the pulpit, with a purpose never to come down its steps until he should have spoken words like the above. . . . More than once – nay, more than a hundred times – he had actually spoken! . . . The minister well knew – subtile, but remorseful hypocrite that he was! – the light in which his vague confession would be viewed. He had striven to put the cheat upon himself by making the avowal of the guilty conscience, but had gained only another sin.   (SL 105)

Confession as penance differs from private scourgings in that an auditor responds. As in the example just quoted, Dimmesdale goes through the form of confessing, though the result is never the purgation he assumes should attend the act. 'I am a pollution and a lie.' The people hear the words but, the narrator tells us, fail to understand their true, 'deadly purport,' even though the words affect them deeply, stirring in them the feeling that *they* have experienced sins too horrible for them to speak. Although Dimmesdale supposes that there is some truth he has not yet spoken, which explains why he is misunderstood, the people's response is sympathetic, apparently comprehending even if they miss Dimmesdale's fine point. The anguish and elation that Dimmesdale feels for his own transgression are mirrored in the excited consciences of his parishioners, Dimmesdale's confession having provided the terms for sin by which they can imagine their own deeds. He, like Augustine, is enough of a rhetorician to know perfectly that this will happen: the fact that he repeats the deception often, and eagerly, under the guise of duty belies any claim that he does not desire this hundred-times-repeated sin. The hypocrisy itself holds an irresistible attraction for him, partly because he can find the evidence for his sin – the transformation of 'truth' into 'falsehood' – reflected many times over in the rapturous adulation of his listeners, a confirmation God denies him.

When Dimmesdale says he lies, he is referring to something more problematic than mere misrepresentation – within the limits of his language he does not declare something to be true that is not. The lie has to do with his conception of language as having the possibility of representing to others with perfect fidelity the inner man he feels himself to be. He should be able to insert the amorphous, idiosyncratic sensation into the public discourse. The Puritan discourse, however, would not recognize such vagaries: one is elected or lost; he accepts his place in the historical community or falls away into antinomian exile. The orthodox, those who through ignorance or denial fail to recognize the inadequacy of doctrine, would be incapable of imagining sin except as error. As I have suggested above, the strictness of this code condemns everyone to uncertainty, denying all but the insanely devout a place within the discourse of salvation. Consequently, when Dimmesdale claims a separate consecration for his intercourse with Hester, he produces a division in himself that cannot be represented exactly in his confession. Divided from the church's reality, of which he in his sinless state had thought himself the perfect representative, he can no longer say what he *is*.[7] His deception is in his pretending he could at any point confess the truth of his transgression, and thereby reestablish the unity of his words with his inner self, without abandoning the desire for a private authority. Perhaps his particular desire could be *named*, but because it is derived from its denial of the authority of the church, it couldn't be *explained* within the Puritan discourse. What he does, then, is use the form of confession to arouse that sense of homelessness felt by almost all his listeners and thereby to stir a desire for a return to a unity they only imagine they remember. The narrator calls this appeal to his listeners Dimmesdale's sin.

Dimmesdale is ultimately unwilling to lose the sense of rupture that constantly proves the limits of law: he labors to keep sin alive. Having discovered desire through Hester, he cannot return to the tautological closure of orthodoxy where the proper reader, recall, must be 'transformed in the image of the spirit he set out to discover.' But to abandon wholly the structures of Puritanism would leave only the void, language with nothing to grant it validity, where sin would vanish for lack of a law to transgress. So long, however, as transgression is seen as sin, the transcendent meanings remain intact because they are violated: they are represented in negation. In the myth of sin, truth persists as the lost basis and future hope of fallen speech, and Dimmesdale continues to offer his listeners, and himself, that possibility of atonement. His solution to the threat of the abyss is continually to re-create the limits of the law that he can violate.

To this end he requires the mediation of his fellows, for they provide a normative foundation for language and interpretation. Chillingworth in particular constantly reminds Dimmesdale of the authority of the church and of the standards against which all are inadequate. He is a well of doctrinal clichés, a source of renewal to which Dimmesdale eagerly returns after having betrayed his own words before the people. In his guise of holiness, Chillingworth seems worthy of imitation, seems to confirm the possibility of living within an authentic relation to truth. He is so useful in this regard that his own hypocrisies are never noticed. Dimmesdale needs the sense of the gap between himself and God to motivate his own public deceptions.

Dimmesdale's failure to overcome the split in his desire and the resultant sense of sin become a source of his power as a minister. Frank D. McConnell refers to the relationship of preacher to audience under the Puritan concept of 'edification,' an affective relationship that is neither persuasion nor communication, but an experience of grace in the verbal act. The relationship is an ambivalent one: 'the confessor, in the very act of writing, sets himself as . . . a mediator of grace to his audience; while the audience as a displacement of psalmodic direct address to God, plays a mediatory role between the confessor and the full acceptance of his semidivine status' (McConnell 44). The sin that inspires confession allows him to evoke this moment of grace for which he is both the mediator and the representation. The listeners' experience of the immediate presence of grace places the narrator in that god-like position, capable of joining them in a transcendent unity. This recognition is not a matter of truth; rather, Dimmesdale can use whatever strategy is necessary to evoke that recognition. His strategy is to use conventions familiar to his congregation to suggest their own lack of grace in comparison to his own sinful state: 'The saint on earth! Alas, if he discern such sinfulness in his own white soul, what horrid spectacle would he behold in thine or mine!' (SL 106). They imagine the flaw in his soul to be merely the necessary difference between flesh and spirit and thus can sense through him the desirable possibilities of earthly grace at the same time they feel their own lack of it. In evoking a desire in the people modeled on his own, he reaches that semidivine status: what is divinity if not the power to create others in one's own image?

We do not have many samples of Dimmesdale's rhetorical duplicity, but those few we do have suggest the structure of his sermons. In the following passage, the complex use of negation compels the listener to generate a meaning out of his own theological position. Dimmesdale is attempting to convince the governor that Pearl would be better off with her own mother than placed in another's home:

65

"[Is] there not a quality of awful sacredness in the relation between this mother and this child?"

"Ay!—how is that, good Master Dimmesdale?" interrupted the Governor. "Make that plain, I pray you!"

"It must be even so," resumed the minister, "For, if we deem it otherwise, do we not thereby say that the Heavenly Father, the Creator of all flesh, hath lightly recognized a deed of sin and made of no account the distinction between unhallowed lust and holy love?" (SL 85)

The steady turning of logical negatives – the subjunctive clause proposing the contrary-to-fact 'otherwise,' 'do we not,' 'lightly,' 'no account,' 'unhallowed,' and I might include 'sin' – refuses to assign a significance to Pearl within a sexual relationship. What seems to be suggested is that if one believes God to be 'the Creator of all flesh,' then something sacred informs every birth. By shifting attention away from any moral connection between sexual intercourse and birth, Dimmesdale makes the child ambiguous as a signifier of sin. The child herself, then, cannot mark the 'distinction between unhallowed lust and holy love,' assuming a distinction exists. But Dimmesdale, speaking in Hester's presence, must not seem to suggest that their love has been degraded to a petty lust. The only thing that is certain is the child's presence. The strategy of Dimmesdale's syntax is to empty Pearl of significance: as a sign, she will compel the Governor to explain her existence by supplying the only source of being (God) of which his language will allow him to conceive. Since the relation between the child and its origin is redefined by this suggestion of divine complicity (a gift from God rather than the dire consequence of lust) the child's significance in the community must also change: Pearl is not the sign of sin but of blessing, and motherhood is sacred. By evading any explicit comment on Pearl's physical origin, Dimmesdale can control her moral significance for the town.

In 'making that plain,' Dimmesdale says nothing that would deny his fathering of Pearl nor his love for Hester. The 'sacredness' of the relation between mother and child in fact affirms the consecration of the couple's love even as it denies Dimmesdale's responsibility for the child. The ambiguity that Dimmesdale builds around the child enables him to follow the quotation above with a characterization of Pearl as a penance, whose meaning is as indeterminate as his own flagellations. Once Pearl has been identified as a product of the 'hand of God,' the 'torture' she inflicts on her mother has two purposes: 'to remind her, at every moment, of her fall,' and to remind her of the 'miracle' of the child. The miraculous evidence of the connection between man and God is produced by the 'fall' – the *felix culpa* that the Governor would have no trouble accepting. Finding a moral purpose in Hester's keeping Pearl, Dimmesdale says that Pearl will 'teach her, as it were by the creator's sacred pledge, that, if she bring the child to Heaven, the child will bring the parent thither' (SL 85). By this strategy, he has made Pearl, an expression of Hester's sin, do for Hester what his own confessions do for him: by bringing his words to Heaven through the mediation of his congregation, he will also find his way there. He always insists that his *words* are true (God's progeny), even though he is false.

The elaborate evasions in this passage, typical of Dimmesdale and the text, reflect Dimmesdale's attempt to avoid discovering that the source of his eloquence is not the transcendent, inspiring word, but the desire that arises from his affair with Hester.[8] He must deny the most literal aspect of things (that the A means adultery, that the child required copulation, or that he is a man of flesh) and transform them into the ambiguous signs of a divinity hidden, and thus betokened, by sin. Even in his 'revelation' of his sin to the world in the final scaffold scene, Dimmesdale is careful never to confess to any specific act that might interfere with his role as signifier of the divine. Standing beside Hester on the scaffold, he does not declare himself the partner of Hester's crime, but 'the one sinner of the world!' (SL 180), a title whose universality obliterates the particularity of his act by making him the symbolic vessel of all sin. This move serves only to disguise further the true danger that his union with Hester presents to the community, which is to declare that an authentic union can only be achieved outside Puritan authority. By assuming the role of a *pharmakos*,[9] he represents his sin as the preservation of the society. The effect, however, is to unsettle the boundaries of law even further since his confession always remains inconclusive.

In his final analysis of the letter, Dimmesdale shifts to the third person, further divorcing sin from the particularity of a human act.

"He bids you look again at Hester's scarlet letter! He tells you that, with all its mysterious horror, it is but the shadow of what he wears on his own breast, and that even this, his own red stigma, is no more than the type of what has seared his inmost heart!"   (SL 180)

He moves from the visible cloth letter, the mere shadow of the truth, to the 'red stigma' that is never described in the book ('it were irreverent') and that is even denied by the report of witnesses. But even the stigma is only the 'type' of the mark on his 'inmost heart' (not his heart, but some essential inwardness of that heart), which would itself be still the sign of sin, not the sin itself. Dimmesdale depends on an ingrained association of the hidden with the sacred: the more horrible the deed, the more hidden the signs, which further distract the gaze from the specific violation to the comfortable abstraction of mythic sin. Dimmesdale remains nearly untainted while all are thrilled by his rhetoric.

Dimmesdale leaves Hester as he is dying with a series of statements that, while they tell her to lead a chaste and holy life, suggest that the knowledge of God can be attained only through desire. Hester asks the dying man, 'Shall we not spend our immortal life together? Surely, surely, we have ransomed one another, with all this woe' (SL 181). She still speaks of a personal union that would have meaning outside the closure of the church. She refuses to accept the displacement of satisfaction to the Puritan's transcendent realm, since she still trusts in her private consecration. But Dimmesdale refuses to release her from their compact of duplicity. He tells her to abandon desire, even though she is to contemplate their sin and the law ('Let these alone be in thy thoughts'). Then, as if warning her against deluded hope, he recounts his 'afflictions,' the 'torture always at a red heat,' 'this death of triumphant ignominy.' His sufferings were the consequence of an unrequited desire, which have become his penance and the signs of God's mercy, and I have already shown how he uses penance. He knows, and probably knew from his first moment as a sad man in Hester's arms, that their separate union could not redeem meaning: they have no immortal life together. But what he discovered and continues to exploit to the last moment is the power of desire. He denies Hester, turning his desire into an undirected passion that could not be terminated by gratification, yet he speaks to Hester in the language of passion: unabating desire has brought him to this moment of transcendence. The result of his long trials is that he will now achieve his union directly with the divine. He finds his separate consecration, but it is nicely timed to occur beyond the limits of public confirmation, denying the authority of the church even as he appears to be its martyr. The effect on all who hear is awe and wonder.

IV

Beyond the mediation implied in any narration, this tale's narrator is engaged in a conspiracy with Dimmesdale that is evident in their common rhetorical strategies. Because he is neither a preacher nor a seventeenth-century Puritan, his language will not to be Dimmesdale's. But like Dimmesdale, he undermines the possibilities of language to produce certainty through a repeated narrative device: he describes an event and then follows it with a series of possible interpretations, all of which are more or less reasonable. This wealth of reasonableness does not reveal the truth, however; rather, it displays how meaning is produced, made by language.

An example of this device appears in the final chapter as the narrator recounts the townspeople's various perceptions of Dimmesdale's final revelation. The view most fully presented – that Dimmesdale 'had made the manner of his death a parable' of self-sacrificing mercy – is explicitly rejected by the narrator on the grounds that Dimmesdale's falseness was established by 'proofs clear as the midday sunshine on the scarlet letter.' Midday sunshine seems clear enough and is conventionally equated with the clarity of direct intuition. However, this sunshine falls on the scarlet letter, not Hester's but the 'letter' on Dimmesdale's breast of which Hester's is only a shadow, a letter whose literal existence several witnesses denied in the preceding paragraph. If the sunshine cannot reveal even the letter with certainty, then what 'proofs' do we have of Dimmesdale's falseness? This apparent indeterminacy continues to undermine the narrator's subsequent claims. He sums up the 'morals' of the tale, concluding with, 'Be true! Be true! Be true! Show freely to the world, if not your worst, yet some trait whereby the worst may be inferred' (SL 183). Presumably there is a truth to show, a genuine self, and yet the narrator allows his sinners to satisfy truth with some 'trait.' Dimmesdale's entire experience, however, has shown that when he displays such traits, the worst, if that is the truth, is never inferred. The narrator's signs of truth are discredited by his narrative.

Like Dimmesdale, the narrator addresses his audience from within a conventional form. He is not only the narrator, but the romancer who has invented the tale. His knowledge of its meanings is analogous to the revealed knowledge that a Puritan minister, 'transformed in the image of the spirit,' must be presumed to possess before he can interpret the Word. The authority of his tale is a function of the coherence of his vision. This is not to insist that he make each event into a fully interpretable allegory: the ambiguities of the heart are, after all, his topic; the people may see varying revelations on Dimmesdale's breast. But in the two examples above, the narrator offers interpretations which, although they have the reassuring sound of a hundred homilies, are directly contradicted by other parts of the text. Assuming the narrator did not simply make a mistake, the reader is thrown into an interpretive bind. Either the narrator is the authority on his tale, in which case his claim on truth is merely the arbitrary function of his position; or there is no authorized interpretation. In either case, interpretation has lost its path to truth.

Various elements of the story demonstrate this interpretive bind. In the second chapter, for instance, the narrator compares Hester with the Madonna.

Had there been a Papist in the crowd of Puritans, he might have seen in this beautiful woman, so picturesque in her attire and mien, and with the infant at her bosom, an object to remind him of the image of Divine Maternity, which so many illustrious painters have vied with one another to represent; something which should remind him, indeed, but only by contrast, of that sacred image of sinless motherhood, whose infant was to redeem the world. Here, there was the taint of deepest sin in the most sacred quality of human life, working such effect that the world was only the darker for this woman's beauty, and the more lost for the infant that she had borne.   (SL 45)

Of course there could be no papist in the crowd, but the introduction of this competing perspective does more than simply enlarge the reader's view. It draws attention to the way Hester functions by inverting the conventional relation of appearances to meaning: where a painting normally reminds the viewer of a person, Hester reminds us of a painting. This reversal undermines the purpose of 'Madonnas' (to suggest the unpresentable perfection of Divine Maternity) by forcing us to imagine in those representations the actual women who modeled for them. The comparison is made more problematic by the statement that painters 'vied' to represent the Madonna, turning the devotional act into an exercise of the painter's own mastery. Hester's personal existence is, apparently, less important to those observing her than her presence as an image, an object to be put to work for someone's desired meaning. To suggest, then, that Hester differs from the Madonnas only by the 'taint' of sin points not to the sin but to its sign, the 'tints' of which are identical to Mary's. How can the sinner be distinguished from the saint? Only the conventions of the genre enable painters to represent the divine in paint. Only Hester's Puritan context provides the code to reveal the sin in 'the most sacred quality of human life.'

The paradoxes of the final phrases of this passage do not simply indicate the critical cliché that Hester is an ambivalent figure. Rather, the narrator's language makes her function as both extraordinary virtue and an illicitly erotic physical presence. The juxtaposition seems calculated to inspire conflicting responses of reverence and desire for Hester, the mother and the whore. Hester is not ambiguous in herself; the reader, however, is wrenched between opposing demands of the spirit and the body or, rather, between two intermingled discourses. Hester's meaning depends on the particular interpretive codes the narrator brings to her, and those can vary from phrase to phrase.

Yet the narrator will claim that his narrative rests on the coherence of his vision. As if in doubt that his tale will be believed, he asserts in his concluding remarks that the authority he followed – 'a manuscript of old date' based on various testimonies – 'fully confirms the view taken in the foregoing pages' (SL 183). The striking thing about the passage is not the claim of authenticity, which in its conformity to romance traditions is not remarkable, but the odd characterization of the story as a 'view' he took. It is a claim of perspective, the vision of a unified subject capable of accurately observing an event and recounting that observation in a way that could be generally 'confirmed.' And yet the 'foregoing pages' hardly present anything so definite as to be called a view: the story is a fabric of irresolution that in its muliplicity and systematic refusal to say anything final dissolves the viewer. The narrator's point of view is the conventional foundation of authorial presence, the seat of mastery the reader shares. When the position is unsettled, it disrupts all terms of the convention, inevitably infecting the reader's sense of the interpretive mastery.

The 'Custom-House' section introduces the narrator's voice and its conventions and sets up the interpretive dangers. The chapter centers on the narrator's guilt, deriving, he would have us believe, from having remained too long in the Custom-House. The major topics of the chapter – his heritage, his 'three years' experience in the Custom-House,' his theory of romance, and his finding the letter and Pue's manuscript – are a confession to and expiation of his faults.

The narrator presents himself as balancing between obligations of propriety (respect for both present society and the past) and an improper desire for self-revelation. He is moved by an 'auto-biographical impulse' but is slightly ashamed of the urge (worried about 'violating either the reader's rights or his own') and promises to limit his revelations to superficial circumstances. He offers two excuses for making confidences: the first a desire to find a 'true relation with his audience,' friend to 'sympathetic' friend, though he scoffs at writers who grow too intimate: the second ('my true reason'), to 'put myself in my true position as editor, or very little more' so that the reader will not suspect the 'authenticity of the narrative' has been tainted by subjective distortions. The excuses are not strictly congruent: the half-denied intention of the first is to establish his presence as an individual, peculiar subject who narrates, so that the reader can take his perspective into account; and half-asserted intention of the second, to guarantee that the authority of Pue's manuscript will remain independent of his mediation. This fundamental conflict repeats the antinomian dilemma, placing the narrator between the self-evident truth immanent in the word (the 'trait whereby the worst may be inferred'), and the intrusion of an interpretive view.

The narrator's duplicity is particularly subtle because his ironic self-mockery seems to hide nothing. His failings in the Custom-House, for example, are fully disclosed. In a comic parody of the persecution of heretics (the discovery and torture of whom was intended in part to make last-minute repentance and salvation possible), the young Custom-House officer allows the very old men 'to rest from their arduous labours,' at which they promptly died. He notes:

> It is a pious consolation to me, that, through my interference, a sufficient space was allowed them for repentance of the evil and corrupt practices into which, as a matter of course, every Custom-House officer must be supposed to fall. Neither the front nor the back entrance of the Custom-House opens on the road to Paradise. (SL 14)

The narrator's intimation that an association with the Custom-House leads one to evil is, despite its facetious phrasing, a serious charge. In removing the old men from their places, which they filled without advantage to the state, he forced them to acknowledge the delusion on which their lives had literally been founded. By defining their jobs against his idea of ultimate salvation, he is commanding them to share his perception of reality as the Puritan judges had bent the wills of non-conformists to their own. He can mock his pious days as an officer, realizing now the error of his custom-bound judgment, but the real evils of the human heart, he implies, result from the surrender to conventions.

He describes how close he came to falling to this evil under the debilitating effects of government office and wryly recounts the fates of those who didn't escape: the General, the Collector, and the man bred in the Custom-House. These people do not 'share in the united effort of mankind' (SL 38), a statement suggesting paradoxically that too close a complicity with the forms of society, the 'mighty arm of the Republic,' involves an abandonment of something vital to one's humanity. Each of these three uses the silent space of custom to sleep – mentally, physically, or morally – and is consequently incapable of the transgression that could define them and test the law of custom. They are, ironically, similar in this sense to the narrator's ancestors: they are literal embodiments of the law and hence are ignorant of its arbitrary nature.

The narrator contends that he has managed to escape custom by being expelled from office and has returned to his own 'original nature' to write his tale. This return, however, is veiled in proprieties: 'we may prate of the circumstances that lie around us, and even of ourself, but still keep the inmost Me behind its veil' (SL 7). Nevertheless, he invites the reader to share his genial mockery of those pawns of conventions. If he does so, the reader also shares the independent originality the narrator values so highly. To be capable of this perspective we must, naturally, be free ourselves of slavish custom. It is all very flattering to discover we are capable of this elevated perspective, and the narrator is only to be commended for his attitude. He couldn't, then, resemble his ancestors who used the faith of their people to rule over them with frightful power. Could anyone be sufficiently ungenerous to this pleasant narrator to suppose that he, like those holy warriors, has used his reader's faith as the platform from which he assumes the power to speak the truth?

The narrator plays a game with the readers involving a number of 'Romance' conventions. In recounting the discovery of Pue's document and the tattered A, he begins in the positive, daylight language of pragmatic, empirical reality with a detailed description of both historical and physical circumstances. He notes the 'rigid folds' of the parchment, the newspaper accounts of Pue's death and exhuming, and most importantly the letter itself: 'By an accurate measurement, each limb proved to be precisely three inches and a quarter in length' (SL 27). From the first, though, this precision is limited: not even the embroidery can be described except to say that its 'mysteries give evidence of a forgotten art.' It suggests to him a 'deep meaning'; it gives him a 'sensation not altogether physical.' Clearly, the devices of science are inadequate to understanding, and the facts are little more than an outline on which the romancer must embroider a design 'entirely of my own invention.'

When the great system of western empiricism is abandoned as a mode of knowledge, an interpreter, 'conscious of his own infirmity,' must adopt the rule of romance if he is not to flounder in a lawless subjectivism. The narrator complains that the 'materiality of daily life' (SL 32) in its insistent presence disturbs the faculty of imagination that would give him access to a 'deeper import,' to what he calls the 'spiritual' in things. The famous discussion of the 'neutral territory . . . where the Actual and the Imaginary may meet' develops what amounts to an epistemology in which the imagination, the 'fancy,' is an organ of spiritual perception. Those who spend their lives toiling in a Custom-House of some sort (the majority of mankind) have fouled this organ with an excess of the material world, and they remain in a state of spiritual ignorance.

The narrator's description of his spiritual adventures, however, suggests that he finds his pleasures closer to the earth. Lamenting his failures to produce the stories he had hoped to write, he says: 'My imagination was a tarnished mirror. It would not reflect, or only with miserable dimness, the figures with which I did my best to people it' (SL 30). The metaphor for the writer's task – to hold a mirror up to nature – is conventional enough, but the objects reflected here are not nature. Imagination's mirror reflects only what the narrator puts in it. On the subsequent page the mirror returns, this time a literal mirror in the room lit by the moon and the glowing fire: 'Glancing at the looking-glass, we behold – deep within its haunted verge – the smouldering glow of the half-extinguished anthracite, the white moonbeams on the floor, and a repetition of all the gleam and shadow of the picture, with one remove farther from the actual, and

74

nearer to the imaginative' (SL 31). The narrator's point seems to be
that the distance from the actual that the mirror provides diminishes
the materiality of the room to allow a greater action of imagination.
The normal use of a mirror, however, is to see what cannot otherwise
be seen, one's own face gazing into the mirror. As John Carlos Rowe
has pointed out, the narrator's face is just what is not mentioned
(1229). If the narrator's description of romance is to be taken
seriously, the metaphors must be read for what is so obviously repressed: the romancer's imagination produces an image of the romancer.
The spiritual truths so ardently desired appear to be the narrator's self,
and the 'modes and motives of passion' are forms of narcissism. 'It may
be, however, – O, transporting and triumphant thought! – that the
great-grandchildren of the present race may sometime, think kindly of
the scribbler of bygone days' (SL 37). Perhaps this is the role the reader
is to serve. But if you look in the mirror of romance and see the
romancer's face, have you lost your own head?

'The Custom-House' consistently discredits the common visions of
the world – historical, realist, empirical – so that a reader interested
in what he imagines to be Truth (the secular religion) will accept the
discourse of romance offered to him. But to read is to revise; to understand at the level of discourse is to imitate. And the lure to such a reading
is the desire to see one's own image dignified by the embroidering fancy
of romance. The narrator's offer of truth is an invitation to the
narcissism of the text. On this level the narrator and Dimmesdale come
together: whether their confessions are couched in the language of
religion or romance, they introduce a whisper of desire that entangles
the reader in a complicity with their projects.

V

The dilemmas and duplicities the narrator and Dimmesdale enter
into in the course of writing are problems Hawthorne is unable to
escape. The narrator's desire to write stories that 'look like truth' and
Hawthorne's desire to be read[10] tend to involve other, more repressed
forces of narcissism and the will to power. The fact that Hawthorne
repeats in different forms a similar narrative activity in the narrator
and in Dimmesdale suggests strongly that he was aware of the problem for his own writing. He could not produce a 'sweet moral
blossom.' The book ends leaving the reader with the 'A' ('a type of

something to be sorrowed over'), Hester (a prefiguration of a kind of woman who has not come), and a heraldic phrase on the gravestone ('a brief description of our now concluded legend'), which in fact describes nothing. It ends not with meanings but with a set of signs offered for further interpretation.

I see no futility to Hawthorne's writing, such as might be inferred from both Dryden's and Dauber's work on Hawthorne's entire *œuvre*. Rather, *The Scarlet Letter* displays the intriguing activity of rhetorical forms and genres being mastered for purposes that have little to do with representation in a traditional sense. Hawthorne continually invokes the rhetorical forms that constitute culture, without admitting any language to be an embodiment of truth. The forms allow us the illusion of clarity and mastery when we speak of the arbitrary, chaotic, and transgressive elements of society. I have, that is, been arguing for rhetoric as repression, as the displacement of the dangerous element into acceptable forms. Consider as a final example the first words Dimmesdale speaks. Directed by Bellingham to ask Hester to reveal the name of her child's father, he pleads:

"Be not silent for any mistaken pity and tenderness for him; for believe me, Hester, though he were to step down from a high place, and stand there beside thee, on thy pedestal of shame, yet better were it so, than to hide a guilty heart through life. What can thy silence do for him except it tempt him – yea, compel him, as it were – to add hypocrisy to sin?" (SL 53)

The formally correct and eloquent plea places Hester in a double bind. She can obey him and hold their love up to public ridicule. Or, assured now of his love for her, she can shield him. In the name, he thinks, of love she avoids the revelation that would damn them both. Dimmesdale, it seems, has managed to preserve his power over the community and his power over Hester. 'Wonderous strength and generosity of a woman's heart!' Dimmesdale says, assuming her motives to be all love. But the effect of her silence is to 'compel him, as it were,' to a perpetual commitment to their sin.

Bellingham, the townspeople, Dimmesdale, and Hester all witness the same exchange, and all think they see a display of profound love, whether Christian or romantic. What they must fail to see is the equally profound egotism, the desire for power, that also motivates their speech, for to see it would allow the element to enter that could destroy both personal and communal relations. The reader is also invited into the seduction, which most readers accept: who could, or would wish to, avoid that thrill completely. But he also has the pleasure of witnessing his seduction and resisting it through interpretation. That is, he can witness the momentary lifting of repression as the text reveals its own rhetorical artifice. Hawthorne's narrative disturbs and flatters the reader, but it also allows him, if he wishes, to observe his infatuation with his own desire.

4
Love's androgynous advocates: design and desire in *Absalom, Absalom!*

For all the confession in *Absalom, Absalom!*, the sins of the narrators remain remarkably obscure. In fact, very little of any narrator's life is mentioned: the story is all of Sutpen, and he is not actually one of the narrators. The basic outline of the story emerges in the first few pages, and all from then on is repetition and elaboration. Yet the confessional tone is unmistakable. In part this tone is a function of the dramatic structure: one character is always speaking privately to another. But more indicative is the sense of guilt that informs each narrative, although again the reasons for guilt are not directly apparent. Rather, the evident compulsion of each teller to repeat well-known stories suggests an unwillingness or inability to say what should be said, as if they hide a dark truth, the horror of which compels each narrator endlessly to defer its pronouncement. The purpose, that is, is not to discover, but to conceal.

We tend to imagine that what one strives not to recognize must be horrible or dangerously desirable, but I think there is something here more obvious and less romantic. Confession represses a knowledge of the inescapability of convention. That is, each narrator acts from within certain conventions of class, love, family, and fatherhood that must be seen as having natural authority in order for him to continue acting. Perhaps the most evident convention is one identified by Patricia Tobin as the 'genealogical imperative,' the familial structure by which each is 'guaranteed both identity and legitimacy through the tracing of his lineage back to the founding father, the family's origin and first cause' (7). Such conventions are repressive, but necessary to make sense of the world. They constitute the classic double bind, so that despite the resentment of 'the envious son,' he will participate in them, 'extend[ing] time's mastery' (121) even as he attempts to establish his own power over it. Better, it seems, the double bind than no bind at all.

But that founding father was never there, and the conventions of culture, for all their power, have no natural authority. Sutpen's

78

attempt to establish his own dynasty of design, to become a 'family's origin and first cause' is scandalous, and familiar. It is a transgression against authority, with all its possibilities for guilt, and with all the promise of escape. But it is in Sutpen's failure that the fascination lies, and in the confession and explanation he makes. Like Saint Augustine, he provides a language of desire and transgression through which the narrators can understand the evident futility and repetition of their lives, and through which they can in the process create in Sutpen an origin. Each narrator subsequently invites the complicity of a listener, saying to his listener, you tell my story and try to understand it. For in understanding, each listener recognizes the guilty desire as his own and must confess to another, and so the guilt and confession descend through a line of narrative progeny.

The displacement of familial genealogy into narrative reflects a pattern Faulkner shares with his characters. David Minter's account of the shyly aggressive Faulkner nearly transforms Faulkner into one of his own characters. Dismayed by the meanness of his life and family and the slightness of his body, Faulkner 'assimilates,' 'absorbs' (22) his great-grandfather, the giant founder of his family. Minter compares Faulkner to Rosa, both of whom 'celebrate' the great while 'dismembering' them (22), appropriating the past by redefining their predecessors. Despite their own 'attenuated lives,' the characters, like Faulkner, find 'correspondences between stories they have read, the stories they have lived, and the stories they are trying to tell' (156). So Faulkner renames his great-grandfather (adding a 'u' to Falkner), identifies him only as a writer, and makes him the model of his own fictive giants. But by 'appropriating' the past in this way, the storyteller runs the risk of making it all look like stories, reducing the great to mere fictions, lords of only 'conventional' realms, rather than establishing his own place of mastery – unless the reader can be made to involve himself in writing the story. The complicity I refer to is one that asks the listener to take the teller as an authority, to take the mere penman for the phallic master. The question is how a narrator establishes that complicity.

In the long exchange between Quentin and Shreve that makes up the second half of the novel, Quentin speaks of his grandfather's conversation with Sutpen toward the end of the war: Sutpen came to him 'with that sober and quiet bemusement, hoping maybe (if he hoped at all, if he were doing anything but just thinking out loud at all) that the legal mind might perceive and clarify that initial mistake which he still insisted on, which he himself had not been able to find' (AA 273). In the beginning of Sutpen's career is the plan, an imperative he imagines he devised, though it is an amalgamation of designs he has heard and read. It is a plan that provides order and meaning to his life, resembling in this way the Jeremiad that assured the Puritans that they lived in history, in a purposefully unfolding series of events. Sutpen speaks like a prophet who has seen the way, and thereby can be both original and authoritative. If things have not turned out as he had expected, he thinks that the problem must lie in a mistake, something like the individual Puritan's straying from the path into sin, and that the chaos of his life is only an indication of failures, not of the speciousness of the plan: sin does not eradicate God, a mistake does not negate the plan. And so he recounts his story, 'the logical steps . . . the clear and simple synopsis of his history' (AA 263), to a mind trained in the law, the code that links the equity of human law with the truth of divine order.

But Sutpen never comprehends the depth and complexities of the culture he enters and borrows from. As a child, he learned to value a man on the basis of personal attributes: how much he could lift or how well he could fight. Possessions, such as a fine rifle, were accidents that could come to anyone. When he is turned away from the door of the magnificent Pettibone, however, he finds a world where possessions can define a man, even when he is invisible. Revenge against the absent body of Pettibone would be futile, for even if he could get to the man, he could never get to the center of authority he imagines to command the estate. The structure of property produces the illusion of an originating force that orients Sutpen's desire: he would become that force. Consequently, revenge becomes a matter of formal imitation, the exchange of physical equivalents ('This ain't a question of rifles. So to combat them you have got to have what they have' [AA 238]). Until his death he remains convinced that Pettibone's essence lived in the 'land and niggers and a fine house,' things that can be won by design, 'shrewdness and courage,' and that can be controlled by the law. He conceives of his failure to become Pettibone, therefore, as a legal and logical matter. The legal model is, however, never more than a delusion of Sutpen's. It reflects the desire to close the gap that exists between the material possibilities of the world and the extravagance of his childhood imagination. Sutpen can clear his land, build his mansion, and found his dynasty in his son, but he could never refine himself away to the essential power of a Pettibone who invisibly holds sway over his domain. The literal results are inadequate to his purpose.

Authority demands finally the absence of the man. If a design is finally to mean anything, it must transform all that follows it, creating a world that functions as a sign of the lost origin: a son, an estate, a tradition. For many reasons, the physical world Sutpen produces is always a corrupt sign (because of the miscegenation, for instance[1]) and, consequently, fails to evoke the Pettibone-like image that would enable him to overcome the sense of belated insignificance he felt at Pettibone's door. What persists is desire, and he attempts to represent his design and desire through a narrative that mimics his life as his life mimicked what he thought of as Pettibone's. It assumes that its argument, if logically developed, would finally provide a perfect articulation of Sutpen's desire. But Sutpen's personal tale never vanishes to leave only the perfection of the plan. The gap remains to suggest the monstrous desire that drove Sutpen, a lure to interpretation that proved irresistible. And that ultimately is the point. For his narrative, like his dynasty, to succeed, he must infect another, produce a son of his voice to continue: the tale must become General Compson's own.

This argument suggests two reasons for the inconclusiveness of Sutpen's narrative, neither of which result from an inability (what Bleikasten, after Faulkner, calls a 'failure') to conclude. 'Failure' implies the possibility of success. Bleikasten says of *The Sound and the Fury*, 'failure informs the very pattern of the novel, since the four sections it consists of represent vain attempts at getting the story told' (50).[2] In *Absalom*, at least, perhaps, the attempts are not in vain, but calculated. There are reasons for not concluding, as Scheherezade well knew. Sutpen may, at some level, have suspected that Pettibone was an ordinary enough mortal and that he himself, consequently, could hope for no more. To evade a conclusion is to evade the realization of Pettibone's purely conventional power, or his own.

But we find an even stronger reason for not concluding in the effect of Sutpen's narrative: a conclusion would end the story. Cleanth Brooks's famous notion of *Absalom* as a detective story represents the reading of the book as a search for the hidden source of narrative prior to all speech. But unlike most detective stories, it is precisely the *absence* of any source that gives the narratives their power over the listeners. The illusion of a representable origin serves as a lure, a reason to proceed. Here is what Foucault writes about the power of that lure:

> the original in man is that which articulates him from the very outset upon something other than himself; it is that which introduces into his experience contents and forms older than him, which he cannot master; it is that which, by binding him to multiple, intersecting, often mutually irreducible chronologies, scatters him through time and pinions him at the centre of the duration of things. (*Order* 331)

By placing the listeners in 'the duration of things,' in time, narrative can both deprive the reader of a sense of his own integrated identity and leave him searching for that origin that would orient him but which always '[recedes] into the future' (*Order* 332). The search, that is, paradoxically reveals the contingent, arbitrary position of the searcher: it reveals him as lost. Confession is history that retraces the path to discover the point of transgression where authority became convention. Sutpen, as Quentin represents him, plays on this trap of history, creating himself as the elusive origin of narrative, the model of desire for those who follow.

II

The accounts of Sutpen's life display a conflict between fidelity and originality that occurs along an indeterminate border. Mr Compson, for example, having got his version of the story through the line of descent from Sutpen to General Compson, describes to Quentin Sutpen's first call on the Coldfields where he has gone to get a wife. Sutpen confronts the curious, suspicious town: 'So he stopped again doubtless and looked from face to face again, doubtless memorizing the new faces, without any haste, with still the beard to hide whatever his mouth might have shown. He seems to have said nothing at all this time' (AA 47). The pages are full of 'doubtless,' that double-edged word that denies what it asserts; and of 'seems,' the mark of the limits of certainty. Mr Compson recalls and invents, blurring the lines between Sutpen's history and speculation. The enigmatic figure of Sutpen that emerges through the story fascinates Quentin, in part because the source of mystery has been doubled or trebled: each father supplements the tale, tells it partly as his own. Any attempt to discover a single origin here would be futile. What Quentin learns is not the truth, but something of the strategy of fathers.

In a later section, after Quentin and Shreve have worked for a while on the assumption that Henry opposed Judith's marriage with Bon on grounds of bigamy, Quentin introduces the issue of incest, implying that his father had told him Bon was Sutpen's son.

> 'Your father,' Shreve said. 'He seems to have got an awful lot of informa-
> tion awful quick, after having waited forty-five years. If he knew all this,
> what was his reason for telling you that the trouble between Henry and Bon
> was the octoroon woman?'
> 'He didn't know it then. Grandfather didn't tell him all of it either, like
> Sutpen never told Grandfather quite all of it.'
> 'Then who did tell him?'
> 'I did.'   (AA 266)

The problem here would appear to be a matter of truth: if Quentin is the one who told his father, then the information has no authority. Can we, then, trust anything that is said? Many recent studies of *Absalom* have, in a frenzy of refinement, proved that nothing in the story is certain, perhaps not even Bon's existence.[3] However, what is more interesting than the question of truth is why Quentin chooses this moment and manner to tell Shreve. Since all of Shreve's knowledge of the tale comes from Quentin, clearly Quentin told Shreve one version about the octoroon woman even though he was already aware of the later addition. Yet he maintains the elaborate temporality of the series of narratives, recapitulating the sequence of earlier tellings, including errors and deceptions.

Quentin has substituted the history of stories for the history of Sutpen. The temporal sequence of Sutpen's life and death with its chain of cause and effect that appeals to logical understanding has been displaced by a pattern of return, by the *nachträglich* time of Freudian remembering. Quentin not only withholds information, but disrupts the sequence of events and interferes with the lines of narrative genealogy by telling his father things his father will then tell him. The shift deprives Shreve of the conclusions he had been draw-ing since the path of the narrative no longer corresponds to some original series of events. Historical curiosity with its possibility of complete satisfaction has been displaced by textual desire with its tangled deferrals. Sutpen ceases to be an objectively interesting figure and becomes instead the pretext through which Quentin exploits the fascination and intrigue of his own illegitimate desires. When Quentin discovered the paternity of Bon, he did not simply add this crucial bit of information to his files, but told it to his father so that his father could incorporate it into the series of tales he would then tell Quentin. Subsequently, as Quentin rehearses the tales to Shreve, he leaves in his father's lapses and errors, making his own telling a maze of false leads, concealment, and speculation, which demand at each point yet further elaboration.

The past is always an occasion to perform a confession of one's own lapsed state for another. At one point, Mr Compson offers Quentin a letter that Bon had written to Judith near the end of the war. The porch light is dim and bug-stained, but Quentin wants to read the letter there. Mr Compson does not immediately turn it over to Quentin, however, using the letter instead to speculate on the characters surrounding it:

. . . people too as we are, and victims too as we are, but victims of a different circumstance, simpler and therefore, integer for integer, larger, and more heroic and the figures therefore more heroic too, not dwarfed and involved but distinct, uncomplex who had the gift of loving once or dying once instead of being diffused and scattered creatures drawn blindly limb from limb from a grab bag and assembled, author and victim too of a thousand homicides and a thousand copulations and divorcements. Perhaps you are right. Perhaps any more light would be too much for it.   (AA 89)

The past, Mr Compson would have it, before the modern fall, was a time of greater integrity, when actions sprang unmediated from the events surrounding them. Because people were 'uninvolved,' not tangled with earlier actions, they could be complete in themselves without having to refer to something beyond. Such people would have been almost outside of language; that is, they would not need the complex interrelationships that constitute identity and significane for people like Quentin, but would mean themselves, like a proper name in the mouth of Adam. Mr Compson and Quentin differ from them by having been born into a tangled structure of a blindly assembled, arbitrary meaning. At the same time as he speaks, however, Mr Compson is holding a letter that denies this simplicity. Unlike the flowery, flattering letters that had preceded it, this last message from Bon to Judith inserts them into the entire history of the South. Hence the need for dim light: it is the veil held over the past that lets Mr Compson forget that even during that heroic time, life was a web of interconnecting lives.

But despite Mr Compson's nostalgia for that time of imagined integrity, he does not attempt to imitate its more direct life. He seems, rather, to take more delight in the veil itself. The letter is important less for what it says than as a surviving, if enigmatic, trace of its writer. Everything about it invites interpretation: its missing salutation, signature and date. And Mr Compson's pleasure in the task is unmistakable. He puts his feet up, smokes his cigar, and fingers the letter Quentin waits for, meanwhile providing reasons, details, and philosophies in luxurious elaboration. At one point, he describes the sybaritic Bon as he appeared at the university and adds in parenthesis, '(I like to think this)' (AA 95), displaying not only the enjoyment he takes in the development of his own version of the tale, but the conscious fictionality of it. His power over the tale and over Quentin does not lie in his resolving the question but in remaining in control of the terms of the discourse (here, literally the letter). The past is merely the convention to which he can refer for narrative authority. The peculiar interest of a letter is that it has both its inscribed message and its meaning as something that passes from hand to hand. The second meaning is the more important for Mr Compson, for in that role it serves as a locus of continual transformation and production.

This use of the letter becomes clearer with Mr Compson's history of its progress. It is, for example, Judith's only direct means of entering into the production of stories that constitute her history. She had received many of Bon's letters without understanding them, but this one she takes to Quentin's grandmother. Here also it is the *transmission* of the letter, not its content that is significant.

' "Me? You want me to keep it?" '
' "Yes," Judith said. "Or destroy it. As you like. Read it as you like or don't read it if you like. Because you make so little impression, you see. You get born and you try this and you don't know why only you keep on trying it and you are born at the same time with a lot of other people, all mixed up with them . . . like five or six people all trying to make a rug on the same loom only each one wants to weave his pattern into the rug; . . . and then all of a sudden it's all over and all you have left is a block of stone with scratches on it provided there was someone to remember to have the marble scratched and set up or had time to, and it rains on it and the sun shines on it and after a while they don't even remember the name and what the scratches were trying to tell, and it doesn't matter." ' (AA 127)

Judith knows that the original, intrinsic purpose of the letter is as insignificant as the individual life in itself. Present things (a letter, a life, a tombstone) have no self-sufficient meaning, being inextricably involved with their continuously developing context. They cannot 'mean' at all until they have been torn from natural temporality and made available as a token of exchange. Any mark, any scratch on marble, is simply swept into the past unless it can be incorporated by repetition or myth where it is reborn in the bed of a new consciousness. Judith continues:

' "And so maybe if you could go to someone, the stranger the better, and give them something – a scrap of paper – something, anything, it not to mean anything in itself and them not even to read it or keep it, not even bother to throw it away or destroy it, at least it would be something just because it would have happened, be remembered even if only from passing from one hand to another, one mind to another, and it would be at least a scratch, something, something that might make a mark of something that was once for the reason that it can die someday, while the block of stone can't be *is* because it never can become *was* because it can't ever die or perish." '

(AA 127–8)

The letter's meaning for Judith is in its movement from hand to hand, reader to reader. She knows what many know, that what she is depends on another who must acknowledge or recognize her. What is different here is that Judith demands not merely recognition but her letter's repetition through another's memory. To 'be *is*,' she must place another under an obligation. The passage suggests that Being is precisely this exercise of power over another who will interpret the letter as a trace of what *was*. The effect of Judith's act is that fifty years later Quentin waits attentively for the letter to pass to his hand.

The letter can be a metaphor for the passage of a family name. According to the cultural convention the Sutpens live within, patrilineage orders the family, and virginity guarantees the cleanness of the family line. Patrilineage can provide only the illusion of closure, however, for the familial House must in practice be opened to something like reinterpretation with each generation. The mechanics of reproduction are at odds with the ideals of the convention. The laws of exogamy insist that a man take a wife of different name, the laws of nature that the mate be of a different sex and a different flesh before reproduction is possible. Virginity provides no protection against the 'corruption' a wife brings to the patriarch's blood line, although incest might. Virginity is merely the compensation for the taboo on incest. Mr Compson speculates on the desire for incest that motivates Henry:

perhaps this is the pure and perfect incest: the brother realizing that the sister's virginity must be destroyed in order to have existed at all, taking that virginity in the person of the brother-in-law, the man whom he would be if he could become, metamorphose into, the lover, the husband; by whom he would be despoiled, choose for despoiler, if he could become, metamorphose into the sister, the mistress, the bride. Perhaps that is what went on, not in Henry's mind but in his soul. Because he never thought.   (AA 96)

Henry does not, apparently, ever conceive of physical incest. He is a poet of sorts, creating from the people around him male and female doubles of himself who could consummate his desire symbolically. Love is the theme of Henry's pandering to Judith and Bon, but incest is his purpose. Henry, Mr Compson suggests, desires to circumvent the laws by making a perfect marriage of self to self through the mediation of Judith and Bon, the equivalent of mating teller and listener in a perfect reciprocity. For what Henry does is create from his own imagination a Bon that he presents to Judith and a Judith he presents to Bon, so that their meeting would finally be the mutual re-echoing of the tales Henry's desire had engendered. Henry 'believes' in the authority of the family, but he would violate all its laws to establish his control over it.

Henry's attempt to achieve this 'pure and perfect incest' recapitulates the failure of all tales to achieve closure. Judith's body is no more a simple emptiness to be filled than her ear an exact recorder of his tale of Bon. Henry and Bon conceived of her, Mr Compson says, 'as the blank shape, the empty vessel in which each of them strove to preserve, not the illusion of himself nor his illusion of the other but what each conceived the other to believe him to be' (AA 119–20). But as soon as she takes the step of 'making the image [of Bon] hers through possession' (AA 95), by sacrificing the illusion of virginity, she would take the tale from Henry to make it her own. This is Henry's naiveté. But for Mr Compson, Henry's failure to account for Judith's revisionary role in the tale (much less Bon's) provides the space he needs to elaborate upon Henry's attempt to achieve that incestuous 'communion with the self,' as Kenneth Burke terms it.[4] It provides the interpretive riddle (incest) that Mr Compson knows would most fascinate his Quentin.[5]

Mr Compson provides one line of narrative that comes to Quentin, Rosa Coldfield the other. Through his tale of Henry, Mr Compson represents narrative as the narcissistic self-communion of incest that attempts to end all stories. Rosa represents nearly the opposite, the self-effacing denial of a desire that persists only by perpetuating itself through others. She is a model, as Minter suggests, for those living the attenuated lives following a time of giants – for Faulkner after his great-grandfather, for Hawthorne after his steeple-crowned ancestors. Despite the petty and sordid events that may literally have filled those lives, as stories they provide a magnificent design for life that fills those who follow with envy and desire. Rosa is not the object but the messenger of desire.

The story she tells is not about a man named Bon, but about the capacity of a signifier, a name, to generate a narrative under the pressure of desire. Rosa, the child who follows Bon's career without ever seeing him, receives his seed more surely than the placid Judith. To Rosa, the word 'Bon' was pure significance:

(I never saw him. I never even saw him dead. I heard a name, I saw a photograph, I helped to make a grave; and that was all) . . . Yet on the day when I went out there to stay that summer, it was as though that casual pause at my door had left some seed, some minute virulence in this cellar earth of mine quick not of love perhaps (I did not love him; how could I? I had never even heard his voice, had only Ellen's word for it there was such a person).
(AA 146)

The word that Bon leaves in the house is sufficient to generate a 'fairy-tale' expressive of Rosa's desire precisely because it has no concrete referent. It is a locus upon which Rosa can elaborate, to create (as Henry had done) an image of Bon out of her own desire.

The source of Rosa's desire is the desire she imagines Judith must feel for him. Her situation recalls Lacan's claim that all desire is the desire of the other: desiring what another (Judith) whom she admires intensely desires, she transforms the object to make it worthy of her love. Such transforming power does not depend on the intrinsic value of the man: it creates what it needs.

But I never saw it [Bon's face]. I do not even know of my own knowledge that Ellen ever saw it, that Judith ever loved it, that Henry slew it; so who will dispute me when I say. Why I did not invent, create it? – And I know this: if I were God I would invent out of this seething turmoil we call progress something (a machine perhaps) which would adorn the barren mirror altars of every plain girl who breathes with such as this – which is so little since we want so little – this pictured face. I would not even need a skull behind it: almost anonymous, it would only need vague inference of some walking flesh and blood desired by someone else even if only in some shadow-realm of make-believe. – A picture seen by stealth.
(AA 147)

The man is unimportant beside the fact that Judith desired him. From that point on, desire works almost like a 'machine' to produce its object. The picture does not require a living man behind it (a 'vague *inference*' suffices, i.e. the interpretive action of the viewer). And even the *desire* of someone else need be only a fiction, for the girl Rosa knows only the signs of desire: Judith and her desires are mere supposition ('as Judith loved him, or as we thought she did,' AA 147). The girl creates not only the desired man but also the desiring rival.

Two aspects of the mechanism of desire appear in the description. One is the placement of the picture against her own reflected image in the 'mirror altar,' altering by juxtaposition both reflected and photographic images. As in the pool of Narcissus, both her own reflection and the image of the beloved appear in a single glance. The second is the association of Bon with the futility and guilt of choosing, like Kierkegaard's editor 'A' above, an object both illegitimate and unattainable ('A picture seen by stealth'). Built as it is of the tales passed from Henry through Judith, a fantasy born of fantasies, her desire has no object to pursue, no course but to perpetuate the production of love's tale: Rosa 'became not mistress, not beloved, but more than even love: I became all polymath love's androgynous advocate' (AA 146). The lover and beloved still dream of possession, of the consummation that should grant each virgin lover the other's being, each dreaming that they will quiet their desire with love's plenitude. For the lovers, love is a finality, the end rather than the form of desire, as if by presenting themselves with humility before the bar of love's court they would be granted the justice of their plea. The child, however, excluded from love's hopes has only love's plea: she is 'advocate,' love's legal mind, who lends her knowledge of the formal nature of love to the lovers' conspiracy. Like Mr Compson listening to Sutpen, she hears the design of desire, not the impossible designs of dynasty and love that Sutpen and Judith see. And she returns it to Judith. She says:

[I was] child enough to go to her and say 'Let me sleep with you'; woman enough to say 'Let us lie in bed together while you tell me what love is,' yet who did not do it because I should have had to say 'Don't talk to me of love but let me tell you, who know already more of love than you will ever know or need.' (AA 148)

Rosa is Eros (Rose/Eros?). She does not represent love's fulfillment but the moving point of desire between hope and its object. As 'advocate,' she is the third element that (like Plato's Eros of *The Symposium*) goes between the signifier and its truth, creating desire.

At the heart of Rosa's narrative is something like the myth of the fall with her subsequent emergence into a guilty language. The desired end, the 'what-is-to-be' (AA 142) that is always just beyond the veil, quite explicitly emerges from pre-articulate memories, but she can only conceive of it as already lost:

> but is that true wisdom which can comprehend that there is a might-have-been which is more true than truth, from which the dreamer, waking, says not 'Did I but dream?' but rather says, indicts high heaven's very self with 'Why did I wake since waking I shall never sleep again?'   (AA 143)

The value of the 'might-have-been,' like the idea of Bon, derives from its freedom from the degradation of repetition and translation since it is beyond hope of presentation. The lines recall Caliban's regret at waking: 'in dreaming,/The clouds methought would open and show riches/Ready to drop upon me, that when I waked,/I cried to dream again' (*Tempest*, III, iii, 145–8); and he curses Prospero for having taught him language, the real awakening. The might-have-been marks the moment when consciousness intrudes upon experience so that from then on all is mediated by language. Although that past could be consciously known only after one had waked to the language that can name it, there remains a regret that such silent sleep cannot be regained, even to the point of 'indicting high heaven' – Lucifer's resentment upon discovering his sense of self-creation is a delusion.

The forms Rosa invokes are literary archetypes. Her desires, she suggests, transcend any individual circumstance. Her summer of wisteria is 'every female's who breathed above dust' (AA 144). It is the other side of Mr Compson's idea of virginity: he refers to the empty vessel to be filled, while she alludes to the 'bride of quietness' (Keats's urn) 'When the entire spirit's bent is one anonymous climaxless epicene and unravished nuptial' (AA 145). Where Henry longs for a hermetic incest, Rosa longs for an unconsummated marriage to relieve her 'virgin's itching discontent' without the loss that is the cost of ravishment. The base of her desire is as narcissistic as Henry's: claiming to have 'heired' (erred) from 'all unsistered Eves since the Snake,' she associates her desire with Eve's to possess the god-like power of self-creation and self-identity.

Rosa's power as a narrator is to exploit the tradition of desire, both sexual and metaphysical, to motivate her narratives, first of Bon, then Sutpen. Judith's desire had initiated Rosa (as Johannes's desire initiated 'A' above), and now Rosa uses her own desire to arouse an imitative passion in Quentin. In her story, the urn-like desire is prepared precisely so that Sutpen can speak the sentence that will shatter it – he proposes a trial mating with Rosa to test her capacity to produce a son, a proposal to smash the urn to see its contents. Her response is to deny him and to usurp his sentence for her own discourse. When she finally tells Quentin of the event, it is not to explain but to draw him into the task of interpreting Sutpen:

> I will tell you what he did and let you be the judge. (Or try to tell you . . . It can be told; I could . . . repeat the bold blank naked and outrageous words just as he spoke them, and bequeath you only that same aghast and outraged unbelief I knew when I comprehended what he meant; or take three thousand sentences and leave you only that Why?, Why?, and Why? that I have asked and listened to for almost fifty years.) But I will let you be the judge and let you tell me if I was not right. (AA 166–7)

She is not interested in indicting Sutpen or representing him. His significance, and his transgression, were no more than she had already to fit into her own design. She understands what she in some way already knew, and for which therefore she already felt guilty. Her compulsion to repeat Sutpen's transgression denies her own complicity, while it retains the event's scandalous excitement. It is this mixture of knowledge and denial she can transfer to Quentin: it is her requital and revenge.

III

Quentin bears the confluence of the narrative streams of Mr Compson and Rosa to Shreve. The two boys remember and create an early history for Sutpen as part of a 'game': 'You wait. Let me play a while now' (AA 280), says Shreve at one point. The dialogue is a self-conscious dialectic, each speaker continuing and appropriating the other's narrative. The story they tell is not an explanatory history of how Sutpen got to his Hundred, but of how he learned and then attempted to master the myths of family and dynasty, first as he lived them and then again as he recounted them to General Compson. Sutpen had to learn and then reconstruct the terms of the success he desired. The story Quentin teaches to Shreve is a paradigm of

Quentin's own attempt to master the conventions he grew up within and to reproduce them on his own terms.

The period prior to Sutpen's encounter with Pettibone's doorman has no temporal dimensions and no history. Sutpen's life in the mountains and his family's long migration to the coast are narrated in vague terms without specific times or places. The land 'belonged to anybody and everybody' (AA 224); the events of Sutpen's life were too undifferentiated to form more than the roughest chronology. For Sutpen, all life and time were identical to his own, differing only insignificantly by quantity, not essence: 'he did not even imagine then that there was any such way to live [like the Tidewater rich] or to want to, or that there existed all the objects to be wanted which there were, or that the ones who owned the objects . . . could look down on the ones that didn't' (AA 221). He has no categories of understanding that could include others different from himself and hence no idea that he lacked anything, no sense of hierarchy. He still has no concept of a discrete self, as if he had no 'I' to set him apart from the rest of the world. Desire could not be a part of Sutpen yet because nothing was absent, nothing lacking that might satisfy him. He would not imagine trying to obtain any object that had not come naturally, by luck, to him. Things happened around him but not to him, and thus not even his memories of that time belong to him. That past does not exist until, as an old man, his oral reconstruction of it becomes necessary to account for the failure of his plan, to try to discover the mistake in his design. Because the loss that torments him must, he thinks, have some origin, the only way he might regain the clear vision prior to the error is by re-creating his life.

The first signs of consciousness, and these still before he had lost his innocence (AA 228), are aroused by the treatment of his father, laughed at and jeered from a tavern as they travel down the mountain: 'He had learned the difference not only between white men and black ones, but he was learning that there was a difference between white men and white men . . . without being aware of it yet' (AA 226). The difference between one rifle and another or one arm stronger than another he could see, but these were accidental differences, perceptible and measurable. The men who jeered his father, though, seemed to see essential differences between people, qualities detectable only by signs he had not yet begun to read or even to know were signs. Because hair, clothing, and shoes were things anyone could alter (by 'experimenting with a comb,' for instance), he could not imagine they meant anything.

When he reaches the tidewater, he approaches the house of Pettibone, epitome of plantation aristocracy, unable to imagine a situation
in which Pettibone will be more or less than he, except by a countable
number of possessions. But that difference could not justify his being
turned away from the front door. He is unable to comprehend the
motivation for the act: anyone going to the rear of his house, he
reasons, 'would be either hiding or escaping, neither of which he was
doing' (AA 223). Without knowing what it is that he does not have, he
feels its loss simply because he has been denied. Consciousness and the
motivated action that derives from consciousness begin with the experience of loss and desire. 'He would have to do something about it in
order to live with himself for the rest of his life' (AA 234), but cannot yet
know what to do.

Sutpen's strategy for escaping the line of condescension that made
him an indistinguishable part of a class that he had not even realized
was a class is to duplicate the man who had introduced him to difference. The man Pettibone himself, however, never actually appears
to Sutpen, but always exists inside the house, behind the house slave,
'seeing them all the time.' Sutpen, as Sutpen, does not exist until he
sees the house seeing him. But with that act he also creates Pettibone as
the rival to be imitated. Desire enters Sutpen when he first interprets
the effects of wealth as the source of potency. As Kartiganer points out,
Sutpen is a 'literalist of the imagination, blind to the arbitrary nature of
symbols in society' (90). Sutpen takes the signs of authority for a
natural code when they are in fact socially determined. This is a
misinterpretation analogous to the *méconnaissance* Lacan describes by
which the child decides the father's penis is the source of his power,
thereby transforming the physical object into the symbolic phallus.[6]
The mistake leads the child into an extended confusion of the true
forms of power and a pursuit of the illusory symbol. Sutpen's initial
disappointment stemmed from having believed that the door to the
house could have been opened to disclose the man standing up inside;
what he discovers is that the man is accessible to him only through his
own imitation of authority's effects. He is seduced by the house, which
told the history of Pettibone's success.

The history of Pettibone, however, will be a new tale when retold
through the person of Sutpen; for Sutpen's ignorance of the conventions that surround Pettibone forces him to translate the signs of
Pettibone's authority into either his mountain idiom or the clichés

of the little literature he had acquired during his time in school when his teacher read aloud:

> He told Grandfather, 'I learned little save that most of the deeds, good and bad both, incurring opprobrium or plaudits or reward either, within the scope of man's abilities, had already been performed and were to be learned about from books. So I listened when he would read to us. I realize now that on most of these occasions he resorted to reading aloud only when he saw that the moment had come when his entire school was on the point of rising and leaving the room. But whatever the reason, he read to us and I anyway listened, though I did not know that in that listening I was equipping myself better for what I should later design to do than if I had learned all the addition and subtraction in the book. That was how I learned of the West Indies. Not where they were . . . [but] that there was a place called the West Indies to which poor men went in ships and became rich, it didn't matter how, so long as that man was clever and courageous.'   (AA 241–2)

His initial perceptions, then, about the man he supposed to live behind Pettibone's door were prepared by having heard the tales of great deeds. It was not Pettibone's wealth that appealed to him, but that wealth gave material form to a kind of desire the tales of the West Indies planted in him. The task of seduction had already been initiated by the teacher, who had learned that the physical discomfort of his class, like Rosa's 'itching discontent,' could be displaced through the channels of the story. He created disembodied desire out of bodily unrest, redirecting a simple desire to move into a desire to move to 'the West Indies.' Pettibone supplied a reference for the necessarily vague claims of the text.

This narrative that Quentin and Shreve tell is built around the repeated failures of an innocent to recognize and adapt to the conventions of the world he moves through. Sutpen's design is merely his attempt to interpret the conventions, but because he comes from a different class, almost a different world, the stories suffer a radical translation. The story of Sutpen's development does not describe a simple amassing of wealth, but his mastering of the language of the school teacher's story, absorbing the romantic world the teacher related into his own literal idiom.

Before he leaves for Haiti, he demands proof from his teacher that the stories he had read were true, assuming that the language must correspond to some reality as he understood it, to which the teacher responds 'Didn't you hear me read it from the book? – "How do I know what you read was in the book?" I said' (AA 242). At this point he is already skeptical about the connection between language and truth, but has not yet discovered where in the path of signification the break might occur: in his listening, in the teacher, in the book? 'Haiti' is sheer promise, a hope without substance or location ('Not where they were') or any means of fulfillment; so that when Sutpen, telling the story of his flight, says, 'So I went to the West Indies,' without any further details, his story reflects the limitations of the teacher's book: the goal is achieved in Sutpen's narrative with the same declarative act by which he had first heard of the goal. It is as if he had been still too innocent when he made his journey to have realized that the means of his getting to Haiti had a story too, because the book had not granted importance or even existence to such necessities. Hence he retains no verbal memory of the act: it had no place in the history.

As Quentin tells it, the literal world inhabited by real men is less important to Sutpen's design than the narrative revision: '. . . he was not talking about himself. He was telling a story' (AA 247). He does not need to present a correct representation of his life's events: he is creating a figure of authority equivalent to the Pettibone he imagined. Such authority requires the disruption of prior histories: Sutpen must distinguish himself, make a figure of himself different from that granted him by his predecessors. It is an ahistorical impulse of modernity, an impulse apparent in Quentin's narrative.[7] When the literal becomes literary, it breaks the conventional order of signification and introduces a degree of play into the terms. Sutpen, at the end of a line of Sutpens, could never effect the break necessary to make his story match Pettibone's without the violence of the literary. He may use the language of Pettibone and the school teacher, but he redefines it. For example, in Sutpen's design success is granted by definition to those who are 'courageous and shrewd.' The Compsons translate: 'he did not mean shrewdness. . . . What he meant was unscrupulousness only he didn't know that word because it would not have been in the book from which the school teacher read. Or maybe that was what he meant by courage' (AA 250). Authority over language does not belong to one who employs it too literally, too 'scrupulously,' but to one who suits it to his needs. Sutpen does *mean* shrewdness, though his sense of meaning does not suit the legal mind. To Sutpen, shrewdness and courage mean the difference between master and slave, strong and weak, rich and poor. Sutpen does not find the criterion of scrupulousness significant. The scrupulous man is the slave of the strong; the shrewd and courageous man commands his own terms: 'he went out and subdued them' (AA 254). Language is Sutpen's power. He had learned to speak a new language in order to control the slaves, first in Haiti and later on his own land. Language is his access to the history that follows him.

Quentin recalls a time with his father when listening had become no longer necessary:

> because you knew it all already, had learned, absorbed it already without the medium of speech somehow from having been born and living beside it, with it, as children will and do: so that what your father was saying did not tell you anything so much as it struck, word by word, the resonant strings of remembering. (AA 212–13)

Words do not 'tell you anything.' The tale does not represent an event, but evokes another tale, each word referring only to another word. Insofar as Sutpen has shaped those words, he constitutes the memory of those who follow him. When Quentin's grandfather, telling of Sutpen, speaks of language as 'that meager and fragile thread . . . by which the little surface corners and edges of men's secret and solitary lives may be joined for an instant now and then' (AA 251), he is misunderstanding the power Sutpen's words have over him. The illusion of being joined to another is a consequence of men's 'secret and solitary lives' being conditioned by the memories they are given in stories. Sutpen, having tuned the 'strings of remembering,' makes all songs partly his own.

Although this condition constrains Quentin, it is also his power. When he tells Sutpen's story to Shreve, he imitates even the temporality of Sutpen's tellings, an aspect central to the seductive power in the tale. He comes to the point of Sutpen's Haitian marriage and says,

> 'Then he stopped.'
> 'All right,' Shreve said, 'Go on.'
> 'I said he stopped,' Quentin said.
> 'I heard you. Stopped what?' (AA 255)

And Shreve launches upon a series of questions about how Sutpen could have managed his Haitian dilemmas, insisting that the story's logic demands more events to have gotten Sutpen to Mississippi. The gaps in the tale compel Shreve to pursue an expected integrity, a temporal coherence of the story that will permit him to conceive of

Sutpen's having *stopped*. Quentin, having drawn this response by his own stopping, explains, 'He stopped talking, telling it,' leaving the ambiguous 'it.'

'He just said that he was now engaged to be married,' Quentin said, 'and then he stopped telling it. He just stopped, Grandfather said, flat and final like that, like that was all there was, all there could be to it, all of it that made good listening from one man to another over whiskey at night. Maybe it was.'

The 'it,' which refers both to the Haitian adventure and to the recounting of the deeds, suggests the sliding that always exists between the tale as a representation of the past and the tale as telling in itself. And thus the deferral within the tale seems to have introduced an omission, a failure that might be rectified if the listener only prompts his informant to elaborate. The effectiveness of the seduction for both Sutpen and Quentin depends on shifting attention away from themselves as speakers, diminishing their presence in the narrating. Sutpen had told the tale as if 'he was just telling the story about something a man named Sutpen had experienced' (AA 247), in a 'pleasant faintly forensic anecdotal manner . . . detached and impersonal' (AA 250), effacing himself personally from the events of the tale. And similarly, Quentin speaks in a 'flat, curiously dead voice' (AA 255 & 258), different from Sutpen's, but providing the same illusion of withdrawal: the speakers transfer what is personal in the narrative from the voice to the structure of the tale itself. The impersonality serves the same purpose in both cases of engaging the listener with the story rather than with the speaker as subject, causing (not allowing) 'Shreve to watch him from the beginning with detached speculation and curiosity' (AA 155–6). The speaker creates the legal mind of the listener, drawing him out of a relation of passive, sympathetic response into interpretation, drawing Shreve into the Compsons' discourse on Sutpen.

The voice that Shreve finally speaks in when he takes up the narrative is, consequently, indistinguishable from the series of fathers. 'He sounds just like father,' Quentin says repeatedly (AA 181, 207, 211), just as Quentin too is accused of sounding 'like [his] old man' (AA 261). Quentin thinks,

Maybe we are both Father. Maybe nothing happens once and is finished . . . Or maybe Father and I are both Shreve, maybe it took Father and me both to make Shreve and Shreve and me both to make Father or maybe Thomas Sutpen to make all of us.   (AA 261–2)

In this passage, the direction of propagation is lost: it can no longer be said that son follows father, that the latest listener follows the speaker. Priority and sequence are confused in a complex of telling and retelling, creation and repetition: consider again how Quentin had to tell his father about the incest in order to hear it from him (AA 266). The two boys are linked: 'all boy flesh that walked and breathed stemming from that one ambiguous eluded dark father-head and so brothered perennial and ubiquitous everywhere under the sun' (AA 299). That patriarchal figure is not Mr Compson, not even Sutpen, but some mythic 'father-head' that allowed Sutpen to imagine Pettibone and the boy to imagine Sutpen. They are all brothered by their belatedness to this father. Thus Shreve can enter the dialogue with no personal psychological commitment: he must merely, like Sutpen, continue repeating 'the clear and simple synopsis of his history' (AA 263).

Faulkner apparently intended the voices of the two boys, Quentin and Shreve, to maintain distinctions of latitude – 'differences not in tone or pitch but of turns of phrase and usage, of words' (AA 303) – but except for an intermittent colloquialism imposed upon Shreve ('You give me jack as I want it,' [AA 300]) his voice and words are wholly interchangeable with those of the other speakers. So eminent an authority as Irving Howe acknowledges this resemblance as the 'drone of eloquence' (225). What emerges in Faulkner's writing is the similarity of two speakers who have ceased to maintain a clear division of speaker and listener and yet who, not having merged, create their tale between them:

> both thinking as one, the voice which happened to be speaking the thought only the thinking become audible, vocal; the two of them creating between them out of the rag-tag and bob-ends of old tales and talking, people who perhaps had never existed at all anywhere, who, shadows, were shadows not of flesh and blood which had lived and died but shadows in turn . . .
>
> (AA 303)

Thinking here has become indistinguishable from talking-listening. The two exist as themselves only in the language ('free of flesh,' we are told [AA 295]), and the only past is the words in 'rag-tag and bob-ends of old tales.' With this doubling of Quentin and Shreve, a metaphor that has underlain every history of Sutpen's family becomes manifest: the creation of the tale depends on a speaker's desire to marry his voice to a projection of himself, the most 'pure and perfect incest.'

With Quentin and Shreve, the act of telling merges with the story being told. The two speak of Henry and Bon riding together from the war back toward Sutpen's Hundred: 'It did not matter . . . which one had been doing the talking. So that it was not two but four of them riding two horses through the dark. . . . four of them and then just two – Charles-Shreve and Quentin-Henry' (AA 334). Two narrative operations are at work. One works between past and present, by which Quentin creates a Henry who shares his subjectivity. The other operation reflects the intersubjectivity of Quentin and Shreve, 'both thinking as one.' Intersubjectivity, as Lacan describes it, is a sharing of the unconscious element of speech, by which he means something 'not at the disposal of the subject in re-establishing the continuity of his conscious discourse' (*Écrits* 49). What Lacan suggests is that two people can share something in speech that is independent of representation. The narrative produced in the attempt to present a coherent history contains an 'unconscious' element independent of the story's particular details. In telling Henry and Bon's story as if it were their own, Quentin and Shreve do more than collapse the two histories: they also produce that 'transindividual' element that weds them linguistically on a level over which they finally have no control.

This intersubjective aspect of language is analogous to the paternal legacy of familial resemblance in all the speakers; incest would be the attempt to make that paternity fully present, manifest to consciousness. Incest involves a desire to make the past ('the shadow of whose absence my spirit's posthumeity has never escaped,' says Bon, [AA 317]) available to be known ('penetrated') and thereby mastered. The thoughts and features Henry and Bon share (though 'obscured a little by that alien blood' of the mother) are the signs of their father's presence in both of them. But it is just that degree of resemblance that reminds them of how much of the father Bon and Henry do not possess. Their talking seems to be an attempt to refine away the differences between them so that an absolute family knowledge might be left. Quentin and Shreve imagine Bon and Henry 'submerged in the bright unreal flood of Henry's speech' (AA 318) as they discuss Judith, but the flood does not dissolve the differences. Between speaking and hearing comes a gap, a fault – 'faultings both in creating the shade whom they discussed . . . and in hearing and sifting and discarding the false and conserving what

99

seemed true, or fit the preconceived' (AA 316). Both Bon and Henry, feeling the distance and denial of their father, want to bridge the gap and possess the sustaining love of that origin, but the path to the father is blocked. There is only what 'seemed true,' only the 'preconceived,' not the truth itself. Consequently, they displace their desire for direct knowledge through a mediating object of desire, Judith, the topic of their conversation. It is only in this symbolic incest of talking that Bon and Henry can approach their father.

But the desire for direct knowledge is only repressed, not replaced by the love object. At the heart of the bond between Henry and Bon remains the deferred temptation to violate the formal limits of the game and challenge Sutpen to make him acknowledge Bon's origins. Bon's desire to penetrate the past is inevitably guilty, for it violates boundaries his mother drew for him before memory. She filled him with her passion and yet concealed its source in his father and the past. Out of his childhood of fierce, fatherless maternal love, he created 'for himself . . . his own notion of the Porto Rico or Haiti or wherever it was he understood vaguely that he had come from,' to which was linked the knowledge that 'you were not supposed . . . to ever go back there' (AA 298). All love and hatred comes to be bound up with a proscription against knowing or desiring to know his origins, breeding in him a mystery based on the horror he assumes his mother feels: 'and maybe when you got as old as she was you would be horrified too, every time you found hidden in your thoughts anything that just smelled or tasted like it might be a wish to go back there' (AA 298). All of the talk with Henry is, however, a wish to go back there, 'to see the man who had made him' (AA 319); it is not a wish to see Judith, his incestuously appealing sister. Both desires are illegitimate, the one forbidden by his mother, the other by his father; yet both prohibitions veil the same object: 'he knew exactly what he wanted; it was just the saying of it – the physical touch' (AA 319). He wants Sutpen's word to confirm what he sees in his and Henry's features, that Sutpen is his father. Yet the truth of fatherhood is not fundamentally a matter of the flesh. As Sutpen discovers in his attempt to become Pettibone, its reality is in the law.

When Sutpen went to Haiti, he had to learn enough French, the legal language, 'to repudiate the wife' (AA 248) he had taken. He justifies that repudiation on the claim that his wife deceived him by concealing her black ancestry, a deception his eye would not detect. The mark of racial difference in his wife was internal, hidden, and yet maintained formally by the law defining miscegenation. One is black no matter how mixed with other races, but one is white only if the lineage is all white. The metaphor at work is that of a stream, which can remain unpolluted only if its purity can be traced to the fountain head. For 'miscegenation' to have any meaning, one must assume the literal reality of a pure line of descent unmixed by alien blood, such as someone like Pettibone could presumably claim with a certified genealogy. But complete knowledge of one's origins is impossible, and only a statement of law distinguishes between one son, well-made though ignorant of his origins, from another who carries the pure line of descent – between Bon and Henry. Miscegenation is a fiction, the purpose of which is to preserve the notion that there is a condition of non-miscegenation, of unambiguous descent. Miscegenation preserves a myth of pure origins, of pure knowledge, of an identity that plunges through the generations to the one father-head. Without miscegenation, it soon becomes impossible to tell for certain who is 'white,' to tell a Henry from a Bon, at which point anyone could claim to be the son and heir of the father. Sutpen clings to the legal letter of miscegenation because he fears his blood line could be infected with a germ of indeterminacy that would threaten his place within the social structure that allows Pettibones their privileged place. Miscegenation, like purity, is a legal fiction that calms the father's fear of what might be hidden in the mother.

Bon, raised by a lawyer who 'did the heavy father,' subsequently studied law. As a child of the law he must understand that both incest and miscegenation have legal and cultural, but not natural significance. Miscegenation had become a meaningful term to Sutpen only after he discovered that Pettibone belonged to a 'them' whose genetic closure excludes all but a select few, all white, the purity of which nature is always conspiring to sully. The taboo against incest is, however, finally in direct conflict with miscegenation. Although incest preserves a family purity, the taboo is necessary to preserve distinctions within the patriarchal family so that the passage of authority and identity can be maintained. Incest confuses the line passing from father to son. At the limits of their enclave, the Pettibones must choose between the purity of incest and the contamination of miscegenation. Bon, renounced at birth by his father, returns to Sutpen bearing the possibility of both transgressions, the one (miscengenation) from his mother's tainted line, the other (incest) from his unacknowledged Sutpen blood, and neither sin can be avoided unless Sutpen admits his paternity. Bon's dilemma is that to gain the confession he desires from Sutpen would be to reveal the merely formal significance of fatherhood when he wants the truth of the father, the potency of the phallus. His solution is to compel Henry to kill him in the name of the father.

The murder comes at the point where the literal nature of fatherhood would have destroyed the myth of the Father. In Quentin and Shreve's account, the murder is the repression of that literalness. Henry does not kill Bon for the incest because incest poses no threat to the myth of the father's pure line: incest merely turns that purity in on itself. Miscegenation, however, would undermine the family design – it is a violation worth killing for. But Henry does not kill Bon to *prevent* miscegenation; rather he kills to prove that he believes in miscegenation and consequently that he believes in purity. Only that act of faith could prevent both him and Bon from having to acknowledge miscegenation to be a fiction, and hence the whole foundation of Sutpen's design to be based on convention rather than nature. If there is no real difference between white and black, the struggle to become the rival and mirror of Pettibone is futile. It would mean there is no determinate origin to the family and no hope of closing it against contamination.

The interpretation of the Sutpen saga that Quentin and Shreve develop depends in each case on at least one character's deciding to act as if the conventions that formed his society were natural. Rosa's faith in the romantic-erotic possibilities of love, Sutpen's in the dynastic possibilities of family, and Henry and Bon's belief in the authority of paternity, lead them to acts that deny the narcissism and desire for power motivating them by asserting the absoluteness of the convention. The conventions themselves are inadequate to reduce the play of various signifying elements to continuous paths of meaning. Paternity, race, social power, love: each produces its sins in the form of excesses that can be controlled only by the steady repression of interpretive confession, but at the same time these transgressions provide the material for Quentin and Shreve to enter the narrative. It becomes their obligation, but also their opportunity to produce their history. On the last page, Shreve carries this revelation of continuous diffusion to an ecstatic limit. He speculates on Bon's idiot grandson, Jim Bond, who escapes the final conflagration of Sutpen's mansion:

In time the Jim Bonds are going to conquer the western hemisphere . . . they will bleach out again like the rabbits and the birds do, so they won't show up so sharp against the snow. But it will still be Jim Bond: and so in a few thousand years, I who regard you will also have sprung from the loins of African kings.   (AA 378)

It is a recognition that his capacity as a storyteller lies in the escape of the Jim Bonds from each design.

In his last words, however, Shreve betrays a misunderstanding of his and Quentin's narrative power. He has, finally, merely inverted the deadening closure of a slavish adherence to convention to reveal an equally sterile openness. It is the formalism of the existentialist glorying in his acceptance of meaninglessness. Consequently he can turn to Quentin and ask, 'Why do you hate the South?' Having sounded its contradictions, Shreve has already dismissed the South and cannot understand Quentin's passion. The question prompts a powerful negation from Quentin: ' "I don't hate it" Quentin said, quickly, at once, immediately: "I don't hate it." ' The point is not that his protestation confirms Shreve's guess, but that it indicates Quentin's need to repress his hatred.[8] Quentin's negation places him within the pattern of repression and narrative that dominates each speaker's relation to the past. His reasons for hating the South are easy enough to imagine; but the South also implies forms of history, legend, and family that Quentin absorbed like the air he breathed. They have become his forms of understanding. Like Henry or Sutpen, Quentin will labor within the form, denying his suspicions that the forms are arbitrary by continuously attempting to resolve the impossible story. For it is Quentin's unresolved (unacknowledged) hatred of the South that leads him to attempt to master it in his own narrative. Shreve seems not to understand that to admit his hatred would lead Quentin to a rejection of the basis of his hatred: his lifelong obligation to hear and interpret the narratives of the South. And that is what Quentin cannot do unless he would risk losing his place in what Burke calls the 'unending conversation' of being in history (Burke 110). The repression of hatred is the source of Quentin's power over his past and over his listener and conspirator, Shreve.

David Minter concludes his biography of Faulkner by pointing to Faulkner's belief divided between something like mortality and transcendence: 'Although one part of him knows "that the end of life is lying still," another part refuses to "believe it's true" ' (Minter 250). Although this may indeed have been the abstraction Faulkner himself would have come to, his own narratives suggest a purpose in his writing beyond humankind's dogged or noble insistence on a truth beyond nature. Certainly his characters seem to have a faith that by pursuing their designs they will create a meaning impervious to time. Sutpen's plan, Bon's paternity, Rosa's love, and Quentin's South – each offers the promise of resolution and hence acts as a hermeneutic lure to tempt every speaker and listener to interpret it. But the attempt to understand can only persist through the repression of the knowledge that truth lies in conventions. Repression, then, is not the blank denial of an evident arbitrariness in life, not a hedge that permits each speaker to retain a faith in man's unconquerable spirit. Rather, repression makes it possible for each narrator to establish his authority in the 'unending conversation,' as one who has violated the law and then confessed his violations. Only the sinner can return with an authoritative knowledge of the law's truth and limits, like the philosopher who has left the cave of illusion. The narrative of the sinner, the confession, can fascinate a listener, implicating him in the narrative.

Few writers have established an authority over the discourse of a history more effectively than Faulkner. Whether or not he would have acknowledged such a will to power over his readers is irrelevant beside the obvious dominance of his language. He has not just revised his own family chronicle, revenging himself against an inadequate father by appropriating his great-grandfather. He has obliged a generation of readers to interpret him, which, as Minter's statement displays, they have done with a subservience to Faulkner's existentially romantic claims that has perpetuated his authority. Only the miscegenation that infects every marriage of telling and listening ensures that ultimately an authority like Faulkner's is not the end of reading, but an opportunity for the reader who can master him.

5
All here is sin: the obligation in
The Unnamable

What the analytic experience shows is that . . . it is castration that governs
desire.   Lacan, *Écrits*

The 'I' of Beckett's *The Unnamable* strives compulsively to finish confessing, to be released from the obligation owed to some 'them.'
There is sin, certainly – why else so much guilt? – but what exactly
the sin was is lost to the past, obscured in a history beyond recovery.
With nothing personal or particular to recount, no secret reasons to
be divined, it is difficult to know just how the sin might be confessed.
And yet the confession continues. This peculiar first person alters the
pronoun 'I' in a way that unsettles narrative at its source, in its
unified history.

Traditionally, and especially since the romantic period, the 'I' has
represented the particular subjectivity narrating a tale. Occasion-
ally, as in autobiographical narratives, it represents the authorial
subject, though more often it is that authorial parody, the first person
narrator (so often unreliable), whose flawed narratives are merely the
openings to the subtler coherence of the narrators' psyches, whether
brilliant or deranged: they may not understand their lives and sins,
but we, reading, can. Although Beckett may begin even his Trilogy
in the midst of that phenomenology so characteristic of modernist
romanticism and existentialism, the 'I' of *The Unnamable* has been
torn loose of the subject. Molloy, Moran, and Malone, heroes of the
first two volumes, write of their own lives' events, few and sordid as
they may be, compelled (as all in the Trilogy are) to represent
themselves for another. But the 'I' of *The Unnamable* refers to no
unified subject, to no single, creating mind that can shape the words
into a whole. Who then says 'I'?

Beckett's language is of necessity enmeshed in a tradition that
perceives of truth as concealed by language's obscurity. Interpretation, motivated by a desire to possess this concealed truth, has striven
toward an ideal of silence, the conclusion of narrative. The greatest

of these truths in post-romantic literature is the god-like author: the existential humanist discovers that when God is dead, man is (a little guiltily) god. The fictional narrator's 'I' is an imitation of and a mediator to the unspoken authorial 'I,' the masterly presence responsible for the book. Beckett's unmooring of the 'I' of the speaker in *The Unnamable* is, consequently, more than simply an attack on the narrative convention. It attacks the very notion of authorial control in a text and deprives the reader of the truth he longs to possess, of the mastery that would validate his own interpretive efforts. The reader is left in the presumptuous position of trying to know what cannot be known.

Almost invariably, however, the recognition that there is no master is rejected by the reader, for it endangers the hope that a successful reading could guarantee his own autonomous being. Beckett's rejection of authorial power, his embracing of 'impotence,' is seen by nearly all those who write about him as potency merely inverted, and his discourse one to be imitated, elaborated, and interpreted. That is, fearful that their own impotence (an imaginary castration) might not be redeemable, they look into the mirror of the text in order to find themselves in the flattering reflection of the author. But their desire to possess the master through his language places Beckett's readers in thrall to what I could call textual desire, an obligation to understand a prior, authoritative 'I' that evades all definition. They mimic the struggle of the speaker of the text to possess the 'I' as his own, which reflects a will to power at work in narrative and criticism, a struggle that recognizes that the only power one truly has over another is that which appropriates his language. The only final escape from sin is to become God.

I

An individual subjectivity requires for its existence an objective world to be conscious of; an *I* requires a *not I*. But increasingly during the course of his Trilogy Beckett denies his narrators that illusion of an objective something to be narrated. The voice of *The Unnamable* has neither a world nor a past self to reflect upon (as Molloy remembers Molloy journeying), nothing to define itself against, yet it continues to scatter the pages with 'I's without an explicit indication that the functioning of the narrator has changed. A succession of first-person singular pronouns seems to demand a single referent. The 'I' of *The Unnamable*, however, lacks the consistent relation to an other, a Not-I that constitutes a coherent subject, denying the pronoun its referential function.

The effect of this ambiguous pronoun on readers appears clearly in writing on Beckett's work. A glance at the major interpretations of Beckett's Trilogy (Ruby Cohn's, John Fletcher's, Hugh Kenner's, and Raymond Federman's, for example) reveals a set of the narrator's names: Molloy, Moran, Malone (these seem legitimate) and the Unnamable, with the capital 'U.' The 'I's of each text need subjects, and the first two novels provide proper names for them; but why would one fix a name to the voice of *The Unnamable*? For all the critics' protestations that the narrator is unnamable, by calling him Unnamable they link the pronouns in a consecutive association, binding them to a unified individual who by the end of his one hundred and twenty pages (in the Grove Press, *Three Novels* edition) has acquired considerable weight and authority. His pronouncements on pronouns, rhetoric, beginnings and endings, and silence – assembled by many critics and quoted as authoritative commentaries on the meaning of Beckett's novel – take on the air of a theory of narrative, ordered, complete in its way, though blind finally to the miasma of the text as a whole. Such is the power of a pronoun.

The attempts to avoid granting the voice a reified self can be quite subtle.[1] They concentrate, as they must, on defining the 'I' as an effect of language, not as the sign of any actual being. In nearly every case, however, that actuality has merely been displaced into some other form – into the continuous, coherent body of the book or into the hidden realm of Heideggerian Being, or into the overarching author who justifies the text's indeterminacies. In such cases, Beckett remains the master of the language, remains in fact his own best critic.[2] This results in criticism of Beckett that is an endless paraphrase of Beckett's own writing, of his inescapably self-critical movement.

Beckett anticipates the subsequent criticism of his writing in 'Three Dialogues with Georges Duthuit' (Bishop 76). The topic of the dialogue is the theory that the impossibility of expression in painting for Bram van Velde is coupled with an obligation to paint. D. (Duthuit, presumably) parodying the sly interpreter asks: 'But might it not be suggested, even by one tolerant of this fantastic

107

theory, that the occasion of his painting is his predicament, and that it is expressive of the impossibility to express?' Replies B., 'No more ingenious method could be devised to restore him safe and sound, to the bosom of Saint Luke.' The existentialist redemption: find happiness in the absurd and grant the unnamable its proper appellation. Although D. seems to forgo the desire for meaning by embracing the irrational, the irrational has become the meaning, and he has shifted the object of desire from an objective truth to the inner meaning that existential man creates for himself. God and meaning are recuperated by an act of will, by an engulfment of the absurd by the ego.

These are the sins against art that Beckett condemns, yet that seem to arise inevitably from his own writing. On the first page of *The Unnamable*, the voice appears to explain the incoherence of his words in the midst of their incoherence:

I seem to speak, it is not I, about me, it is not about me. These few general remarks to begin with. What am I to do, what shall I do, what should I do, in my situation, how proceed? By aporia pure and simple? Or by affirmations and negations invalidated as uttered, or sooner or later? Generally speaking. There must be other shifts. Otherwise it would be quite hopeless. I should mention before going any further, any further on, that I say aporia without knowing what it means. Can one be ephectic otherwise than unawares? I don't know. (UN 291)

The passage is an equivocating, logically empty phrase. Yet the text provides the terms that describe such failures of language – aporia (being ephectic) and contradiction (invalidation) – that draw it back within a rhetorical tradition. So from within the uncertainty and skepticism of aporectic and ephectic expressions emerges, apparently, the self-conscious author in control of his prose, mastering the form of his incapacity to speak with certainty. Like Kenner's clown, 'He does not *imitate* the acrobat; it is plain he could not; he offers us directly his personal incapacity, an intricate art form' (Kenner 33). The lack of meaning turns out to be a sign of strength within an alternative structure of meaning, that of art. This is Duthuit's 'ingenious method' for restoring one to St Luke.

This redemptive reading depends on the control displayed by an authoritative figure. Several aspects of the passage, however, suggest that the speaker is not a single subject, a unified consciousness. The discussion of aporia within aporectic phrases suggests alternatively knowledgable, then ignorant speakers. Does the speaker know or not know? Or does he lie? Of course it's a joke, which is obvious until we lose our sense of humor by reading too pedantically. The clown invites the reader to join him in an absurdity of language that remains funny because controlled by the clown. Call it a joke and the problem is resolved. But if you suspect the clown is not in control, the phrases reveal another force. The term 'aporia,' once evoked, suggests the aporectic loss that generates the succeeding sentences, including the proclaimed ignorance of the form. 'Ephectic' suggests the pointless ephectic phrase. Each word or phrase evokes associated forms: yes suggests no; 'what am I to do' suggests the tense shift to 'what shall I do.' In all of this there is no unified consciousness in command, but only the playing out of the patterns of a given language. The comical figure clinging to the racing circus horse turns out to be not a clown but an actual drunk who has staggered into the circus ring. The 'general remarks' are not the anti-hero's subversion of tradition but the uncontrolled propagation of verbal forms.

The tendency to see Beckett as Duthuit's hero of antithetical art (expressing the impossibility of expression) comes from a desire to rescue Beckett from the unpleasant consequences of his own project. In an oft-quoted interview with Israel Shenker, Beckett is reported to have said, 'I am working with *impotence, ignorance.* I don't think impotence has been exploited in the past.' Most critics find positive implications to Beckett's project. Federman takes the line to imply an 'affirmation of the negative,' 'a substitution of ignorance for understanding,' etc. (*Journey into Chaos* 6). Kenner sees the clown exploiting impotence 'when he allows to bubble up into sustained mimetic coherence his own inability to walk a tightrope' (33). These readings could be readily justified by reader-response theory, such as that of Norman Holland and Wolfgang Iser.[3] They 'fill in' the gap in potency and meaning that Beckett leaves in the text. They allow the reader to find a textual coherence that overcomes the chaos of impotence. Such views make an implicit distinction between the 'impotence' of the characters, of reason, of understanding, and of language, and the potency of the text (the clown, the affirming negative, and Beckett himself). Clearly, what has happened is that Beckett has evoked the desire of the critic by pointing to a possible source of impotence, which impels him to work to supplement his lack with the potent object. In applying the term 'impotence' to the enemies of modernist unreason, they manage to attest to the genius of Beckett's adoption of impotence while ranging themselves on the side of the text that escapes that fate. But in doing so they reveal an anxiety central to the working of Beckett's prose.

Beckett's statement in the same interview that impotence has traditionally been considered unusable by writers suggests less a failure on the part of writers to recognize the significance of impotence than their repression of the part it plays in their own motivations. Lacan may provide a way to understand such motivations in his discussion of the relation of castration to desire. He proposes that the infant, in what he calls the Mirror Stage, recognizes his own reflection as himself, but includes the mother who holds him before the mirror as part of that image. That is, the infant's primary self-representation comprises both himself and his mother: they are a single, ideal self. At the time the child acquires speech, the ability to say 'I,' he recognizes his mother as another, someone separate from him, and he looks for a reason that his perfect bliss (*jouissance*) has come to an end. He suspects he may be at fault and feels guilty; and he suspects some greater power may have supplanted him and denied him the mother. Since there usually is no actual interdiction by a tyrant father, what follows is is a great imaginative act that structures all subsequent desire: the invention of the Symbolic Father of the law. The child thinks the one who has taken the mother and revealed the child's weakness to him must be very powerful – otherwise the mother would not need him. Through a misunderstanding (Lacan's *méconnaissance*), the child imagines the father's power must reside in the most salient difference between the two adults, and decides the mother is castrated. Any subsequent movement toward his bliss (reunion with the mother) is accompanied by guilt for having attempted to possess more than the Law appears to allow, and be a fear that punishment will be added to loss. So bliss is renounced (or deferred) and the child identifies himself with the imagined phallic authority of the father. That is, his literal impotence is tolerable only because he imagines someone else is potent. Because if someone else is, then he too might one day become the Father, reestablish the unity of words and things and find a way to express a demand adequate to his need.

Surprisingly, the impotence that draws one helplessly into futile desire and the subservience to a supposed master can become the source of power. I am not speaking of the triumphs of existentialist man who strives endlessly toward self-creation through a textual double.[4] The power I have associated with impotence derives, rather, from the writer's ability to shape the desire of others on the model of his own. It is not a display of potency, but the perfect control the Father (the 'them' the *The Unnamable*'s speaker continuously refers to) has over his still unlawful desire that assures his control over the other. As Lacan points out with reference to *The Symposium*, Alcibiades 'has not seen Socrates's prick' (*Écrits* 322), despite Alcibiades's offer of himself. The consequence of Socrates's denial is not Alcibiades's ridicule. Rather, in the face of Socrates's self-control, Alcibiades feels guilty and imagines him to be all the more powerful. Any actual display of potency would only reveal that Socrates's phallus was merely a penis. The one who behaves as if impotent (Socrates, the analyst, the writer) invites the lover to fill in the silence and create him as the phallic master. The Socratic Figure, the authorial persona, having lured the speaker into voice, retains, like James's Vereker in 'The figure in the Carpet,' the power either to confirm the subject's potency by taking him into his arms or, more importantly, to refuse that confirmation and ensure his impotence. And the subject remains bound to the task of interpreting the master, a task he cannot complete because the master he needs to articulate is the imaginary master of his desire, an impossible figure beyond all language.

The project Beckett announces – to exploit impotence – is, then, not merely the other side of the Cartesian coin, not the ignorance, lethargy, and confusion that define by negation the knowledge, energy, and order we might eventually attain. Such negative positions are certainly embodied in his characters and rhetoric and in the metaliterary commentary that he incorporates in *The Unnamable*. But these positions tempt readers to adopt those bad readings that recall the writer to the bosom of Saint Luke, ask them to turn the characters into allegorical representations of an existential authorship. Reading Beckett in this way produces devoted paraphrases, curious more for their subjugation to text than for the strength of their interpretations.

Beckett offers such misreadings, perhaps because they reveal so clearly the desire at work in them. In a discussion of problems inherent in dualism, Derrida refers to 'oppositional argument,' 'reflection in the alternative mode whereby the philosopher, at the end of his

deliberations, seeks to reach a conclusion, that is, to close the question' ('Genesis and Structure' 154). Oppositional readings, insofar as
they cannot acknowledge ultimate indeterminacies, are failures: the
desire for conclusion arrests thought under the illusion that the
problem has been mastered.[5] Beckett employs the reader's desire to
think 'philosophically,' but he gives the reader what Barthes would
call a 'text of bliss': 'The text that imposes a state of loss, the text
that discomforts (perhaps to the point of a certain boredom)' (*Pleasure*
14). Rather than confront the discomfort and loss as inevitable
elements of reading, most readers look at Beckett's writing as a 'text
of pleasure,' one they imagine can be pinned down in a convincing
display of potency. *The Unnamable* is not such a work, and the inherent impotence it displays in the readers obliges them to try again
to read the text.

Readers are always separated from an immediate knowledge of the
author, as *The Unnamable*'s speaker is from 'them.' This pronoun
refers to those other voices or potencies just outside the text that
remain undefinable, unchallengable, unknowable. They must exist,
the speaker reasons, since the words he has must have come from
someone else. He feels obliged to speak of them, even though he
doesn't know how to do it properly. But there is nothing pathetic
about the speaker. His cunning is always equal to the task of gaining
his own ends, despite his obligation. Barthes's analysis of readers'
strategies suggests how the speaker uses his position.

> How can we read criticism? Only one way: since I am here a second-degree
> reader, I must shift my position: instead of agreeing to be the confidant of
> this critical pleasure – a sure way to miss it – I can make myself its voyeur:
> I observe clandestinely the pleasure of others, I enter perversion; the com-
> mentary then becomes in my eyes a text, a fiction, a fissured envelope. The
> writer's perversity (his pleasure in writing is *without function*), the doubled, the
> trebled, the infinite perversity of the critic and of his readers.
>
> (Barthes, *Pleasure* 17)

Such reading is, as it was for the writers of Kierkegaard's *Diary of a
Seducer*, a compensation for the reader's losses. He escapes his secondary position by ceasing to read for meaning (the level of signifieds)
and taking up the text in the wealth of its surface, the signifiers. The
text, then, as an object of desire, loses it proper function as mediator
of the truth, as a sign of the writer's potency, and becomes, rather,
the occasion for the reader to indulge his own desire. He is like

Volpone who, in his seduction of Celia, finds his greatest pleasure not in the possession of the girl but in thinking of the excited observers of their embraces. The reader, then, may be able to escape the enslavement of 'criticism,' that endless repetition of the text (the critic uncovering the gems of the work) by refusing the text's offer of satisfaction. Rather, the reader's 'perverse' commentary might supplement the text, producing an addition that appropriates it. As Barthes suggests, 'you cannot speak "on" such a text, you can only speak "in" it, in its fashion, enter into a desperate plagiarism, hysterically affirm the void of bliss (and no longer obsessively repeat the letter of pleasure)' (*Pleasure* 21). The reader forgoes the legitimate *use* of the text in favor of a kind of theft (*plagium*, kidnapping).

This reading is no delicate pleasure that one courts in the subtle flirtations of reading. For Lacan, the desired *jouissance* involves a compulsive return to a remembrance of lost gratification. The perversity that sustains desire is generated not from pleasure but from the fear that if that past is lost, then all hope of meaning vanishes. The reader must resist the pleasurable, but illusory, finalities of the text (the obsessive repetitions) without disrupting the structures of desire that permit him to imagine himself at some point wielding the power to create meaning he attributes to the author. It is, however, precisely in his resistance to the text that the reader finds himself most enslaved to its forms. The reader's initial commitment to the myth of the phallus leads him necessarily to perceive himself in a relation of impotence to the writer's potency. And rather than having proved his potency through resistance, he finds himself committed to the 'fashion' of the endlessly dispersive (hysterical) text. *The Unnamable*'s speaker accepts the obligation to speak, and confesses in whatever voice would seem to maintain the link between guilt and memory. Through this endless impersonation of voices, the book 'exploits impotence' without itself suffering the delusion that impotence exists.

II

The compulsion to continue dominates *The Unnamable*, although the source of compulsion remains obscure. Some imbalance has occurred and the structures of meaning demand a return to equilibrium:

inside-outside, human-divine, self-other must be kept distinct. The speaker does not know when the imbalance began: the speaker, at least, has always felt it. But if the beginning cannot be established, the entire sequence of cause and effect (finally of logic) becomes uncertain. Does the speaker respond to some original transgression and attempt to clarify the distinctions by confessing; or does the language of confession already contain the confusion so that each attempt only furthers the loss and strengthens the obligation to clarify. For instance, the pronouns 'I' and 'you' divide all persons into speaker or others, implying by their presence the existence of distinct speakers. But do the pronouns represent the actual division of people into the self and all others, or is the division a delusion created for each speaker by the pronouns, making him feel himself to be that first person just because he has an 'I' to name it. The analogy with Prometheus that follows plays on the edge of this indeterminacy between representation and invention.

If I could speak and yet say nothing, really nothing? Then I might escape being gnawed to death as by an old satiated rat, . . . the torn flesh having time to knit, as in the Caucasus, before being torn again. But it seems impossible to speak and yet say nothing, you think you have succeeded, but you always overlook something. . . . The fact that Prometheus was delivered twenty-nine thousand nine hundred and seventy years after having purged his offence leaves me naturally cold as camphor. For between me and that miscreant who mocked the gods, invented fire, denatured clay and domesticated the horse, in a word obliged humanity, I trust there is nothing in common. But the thing is worth mentioning. (UN 303)

The futility of trying to speak of nothing evokes, as if by accidental association (rat > torn flesh > vulture > Prometheus), a myth. Although the relevance of the myth is denied, the allusion, once voiced, insist on development. Prometheus emerges through the play of language (as, perhaps, the self emerges from the pronoun 'I'): the metaphors sleeping in every statement can always reconstitute the matrix of the symbolic, that source of endless deferrals that lead the speaker along the path of digressive narratives. In this instance, the speaker's agonizing reiterations recall the agony of Prometheus who suffered without death or expiation; and the myth of Prometheus in turn suggests that transgression has led to the speaker's punishment.[6]

The particular evocation of Prometheus is hardly accidental. The speaker here is a mountebank, a performing liar, enumerating the

several crimes of Prometheus only to claim that his situation and Prometheus's have 'I trust . . . nothing in common. But the thing is
worth mentioning.' Someone, he jokes, may be foolish enough to
make the comparison, but he is not responsible for that. The allusion
evokes a relation between human and divine in which human culture
is the result of a transgression. Nietzsche, referring to Prometheus,
puts it directly: 'Man's highest good must be bought with a crime
and paid for by the flood of grief and suffering which the offended
divinities visit upon the human race in its noble ambition' (Nietzsche
64). The human tragedy results from 'an interpenetration of several
worlds, as for instance a divine and a human': the integrity of boundaries is violated. Prometheus's sin, by giving man (this denatured
clay) the fire that belonged to the gods, initiated the interminable
obligation of man. The fire revealed man's fundamental inadequacy
in comparison to the gods and aroused his need to appease their
wrath. Here, perhaps, is the reason that fire and speech, which make
humanity possible, have become the agencies of suffering: they are
punishments. Humanity was born with the presumption and error of
divinity, and like a psychologically astute parent, the gods punish us
with an excess of what we gained illegitimately. But if there are sins
to be punished, then there must have been a time prior to the sin
when the opposing realms of God and man were not confused, and
there must be an end of time when the boundaries will be re-
established through confession and expiation. Suffering, then, is not
the arbitrary imposition it seems but an orderly 'pensum,' the
speaker calls it (UN 310), a schoolboy's punishment. The suffering
means something: it is a sort of metaphor for the crime and hence
comprehensible. Confession makes sense of loss.

Such, at least, is the line of reasoning that the mountebank could
expect of the hermeneutically acute reader, without himself taking
responsibility for the conclusions. The conclusions seem, in fact, to
be validated, despite the speaker's rejection of them, by their being
embedded so consistently in the language of the text. The myth of
Prometheus enables man to conceive of himself as man by opposing
mankind to a not-man called god; the speaker can speak of his desire
for a self because the pronouns he uses, 'I' and 'them,' allow him to
oppose his self to those other selves. The speaker has prepared for the
analogy between these two structures (myth and grammar) a few
pages before the mention of Prometheus. Speaking of all the others

115

he says, 'I alone am man and all the rest divine' (UN 300). In both cases (the discovery that there are gods; his assumption that there are others to whom he is obligated), the powerful others are the necessary complement to the speaker's own weakness. But these others need not really exist for the obligation to continue. The speaker's sense of impotence leads him to discover the others in his own speech, just as the weakness of the human leads him to invent the gods who make 'man' a meaningful term.

Although obliged to repeat a task given by them and denied the possibility of creating anything original, in short forbidden the satisfaction of *jouissance*, the speaker takes revenge by exposing the others' emptiness through his precise, if mocking, aping of their method. Isn't such mockery always 'worthy of the situation' of a servant, or son? Or a reader? The speaker accepts the words of the other not as truth but as a 'text of bliss' upon which he elaborates in a 'desperate plagiarism' in order to produce his own text. The speaker has said, 'The search for the means to put an end to things is what enables the discourse to continue' (UN 299). It would be more accurate to say that it is by undoing the means to put an end to things, by appropriating and undoing reason, that the speaker compels the discourse to continue.

III

Throughout the book the speaker is obsessed by the thought that he once knew 'a certain highly promising formulae . . . which indeed I promised myself to turn to account at the first opportunity' (UN 308), but they were forgotten. The ceaseless babble by which he fulfills the 'unintelligible terms of uncomprehensible damnation' prevents him from being sure he had heard the formulae. He lingers over the vague memory of these expressions, recalling how he vowed 'never to forget them and, what is more, to ensure they should engender others and finally, in an irresistible torrent, banish from my vile mouth all other utterance, from my mouth spent in vain with vain invention all other utterance but theirs, the true at last, the last at last. But all is forgotten and I have done nothing, unless what I am doing now is something, and nothing could give me greater satisfaction' (UN 308). The *true* and *last* which is forgotten as soon as it is heard is the one object of desire. It offers the illusion that, once possessed, it would reproduce itself ('engender others') to displace all other discourses, overwhelming the noise with its immaculate single note, with a sort of 'nothing.' Within this longing, however, lurks the suspicion that the formulae may even now in fact be present in the text, if 'what I am doing now is something.' That is, the words that first inspired the idea that this true and last state exists are in fact only the futile words he is speaking now, and they have already given him all the satisfaction that is possible, grim thought. The horror of this suspicion, which is never pursued, lies in its suggestion that the speaker already possesses the formulae, or is possessed by them, and that the formulae merely create the illusion of forgotten perfections. The pursuit of perfection is thus identical to this wallowing in language, as if, in confession, one sought grace through sin.

The dilemma is analogous to that of the narcissist caught in an endless struggle to recapture the perfect bliss of the speechless infant. In Lacan's essay 'The Mirror Stage,' he describes how the perfect possession of an imaged self embedded in the looking-glass world is displaced by an alienating 'I.' This linguistic, cultural mark will forever divorce the child from all 'imaginary' conceptions of a completely unified self and place him in an Oedipal contention with the father. The fall into desire, into the dualism of subject/object, comes with the introduction of language and the sublimation of narcissistic libido that results from entering the society of the family (*Écrits* 6). The only return to that primordial paradise would be the guilt-ridden course of supplanting the Father and usurping the unalienated 'I' he imagines the Father to possess.

At one point, attempting to fulfill his obligation, the speaker introduces a name for himself: 'I'm Worm, that is to say I'm no longer he, since I hear.' This has the ring of Lacan's allegory of the symbolic: Worm had Being before the speaking; now that he has language, he has only the name. He describes Worm's emergence into language:

Quick a place. With no way in, no way out, a safe place. Not like Eden. And Worm inside. Feeling nothing, knowing nothing, capable of nothing, wanting nothing. Until he hears the sound that will never stop. Then it's the end, Worm no longer is. We know it, but we don't say it, we say it's the awakening, the beginning of Worm for now we must speak, and speak of Worm.
(UN 348–9)

Worm's Eden, like speechless infancy and the womb before, is the lost paradise where Worm *was*. No safe place exists where the sound that will never stop, language, cannot get in and replace true being with the empty 'I am.' From the moment it occurs, the loss is denied, and the end of Worm is called an 'awakening' – it's the *felix culpa* whereby Adam, in saying 'I am,' awoke to a knowledge of good and evil. 'Worm, he's an idea they have, a word they use' (UN 366). The name is the sign that Worm no longer is. The child says 'I,' which belongs not to him but to language, and he loses the primordial image of the self.

The advent of language marks the moment of the irremediable loss of a self that had seemed equal to the entire world. 'Silence once broken will never be whole again' (UN 366), says the speaker, making explicit the connection of perfection (wholeness) to the absolute negativity of silence. The longing for silence betrays a desire for meaning and presence and a rejection of the realm of empty signifiers. The infant's sense of wholeness in the ecstasies of his full-stomached auto-eroticism, a pleasure shattered by his first 'I,' is prior to speech and therefore unavailable to articulated memory, but the feeling is represented negatively for us in the myth of the fall: once there was perfect bliss, but it was lost when our parents sinned. Because it is tied to the myth of Eden, the very ability to imagine that earliest state of pleasure is tinged with guilt. The myth perpetually reconstitutes the literal speechlessness of infancy as a silence of truth that is hidden behind an equally mythic moment of sin. The possibility that the dim memory of wholeness might be nothing more than the narcissistic pleasure of a satisfied body is veiled by layers of narrative that transform it from an aspect of mere survival into a primal experience of meaning: better to have strayed from the path than to have no path at all. The speaker at one point mocks his absurd desire for truth: 'It's like the other madness, the mad wish to know, to remember, one's transgressions' (UN 336). Even knowing that to wish is madness, he does not cease wishing; but by associating knowledge with transgression, he links the desire to know with confession, the remembering of sin. That is, desire is bound up with a discourse of transgression and guilt: if the place of wholeness has been lost upon a path of transgression, the only return is to retrace the path.

While transgression may have led to a painful expulsion from some paradise, the resulting guilt and obligation allow one to enter the economy of power. Although indebted to a Master, the fact of indebtedness means that the Master must lend his tools to the Servant who, in the inevitable dialectical move, appropriates them. The speaker 'lends' himself to the stories he must tell, making them serve his own ends. Before 'reciting' one of the Mahood narratives, he asks his listeners to understand 'in the way I was given to understand it, namely as being about me.' The listener, hearing and repeating the story, is to understand the story as representing himself, that is, to take the speaker's place in the narrative. The repetition of the tale is therefore not simply a fulfillment of an obligation but an appropriation of the language and the power that attends it.

One story will serve as a demonstration. Mahood on crutches spirals slowly toward the house where all his 'loved ones' dwell. They watch him and talk about him: he's become a 'subject of conversation': 'gaffer and gammer related my life history, to the sleepy children. Bedtime story atmosphere' (UN 318). The children repeat the story, the wife reports the latest news. In short, the life of the entire group centers on the narrative of Mahood's endless gyrations until they all die (of a 'fatal corned-beef'). Mahood the father fulfills his familial obligations and, returning faithfully to the bosom of the family, enslaves and destroys them. The obedient speaker, lending himself to the story, uses the language he is given to enslave his listeners, involving them in their own series of repetitions.

In a complaining moment the speaker laments, 'But this is my punishment, my crime is my punishment' (UN 368). The idea calls up the damned of Dante's *Inferno* who, having taken some pleasure in a transgression before death, are condemned to repeat in a parodistic form the same sin for eternity: because Paolo and Francesca gave themselves up to the winds of passion, they are forever blown around their circle of hell in an embrace that mocks their former ecstasy. But we might also recall the liveliness with which St Augustine retraces his youth's pleasures, or the guilty joy in Dimmesdale's pale-faced confessions in *The Scarlet Letter*, or even the determination of Milton's Satan that once damned he would make the most of it. The implication, which I have argued throughout this book, is that the lament must be considered in its inverted form, that 'my punishment' is also 'my crime.' That is, confession and punishment, insofar as they are representations of the sin, are in some sense repetitions of the sin. The major difference (as Dante's punishments show) is that the original act was incomprehensible as sin (what could Adam know of evil?) while the representation repeats the act within the structure of transgression. Repetition makes one conscious of the meaning of sin and recalls the desire that made the first, irrecoverable sin so attractive. For the essence of sin as transgression is difference, the revelation of a structure of law and perfection that only becomes available to perception when it is violated. The initial transgression, therefore, can only be the absolutely negative action of violation (I will not serve) that reveals the paradise at the moment of its loss – if there was a paradise. There is misery for the speaker, but if the misery can be interpreted as punishment, then it repeatedly evokes the sin and desire of that originating transgression.

Repetition always implies an original. Repeatedly the narrative of *The Unnamable* pushes toward that primacy, conscious that it can reach at best only the second sin (the first confession) and can therefore never get beyond the fundamental indeterminacy of representations: did speech break silence, or is silence merely a myth born of speech; is Nothingness merely the wish for being; is the autonomous self merely the illusory product of an imagined Other. The futility of the task does not, however, arrest the narrative, for it is the genius of the rational tradition to have developed a method of investigation based on the *cogito*, on the 'I' that mimics and reinforces the dualistic oppositions of the universe it examines. The *cogito*, the first elaboration of the 'I,' is as impenetrable a screen to the knowledge of the self's Being as the first sin is to a knowledge of perfect innocence. Reason represents the *cogito* as confession represents sin. In a passage near the end of the book, reason and representation are closely aligned: 'It was to teach me how to reason, it was to tempt me to go, to the place where you can come to an end' (UN 407). Reason does not get him to the end, it only *tempts* him to try to reach the end by representing that end as a reality. But in teaching him to reason, there is no necessary intention to deceive, for the temptation seems to be implicit in the language he learned: 'that's all words they taught me, without making their meaning clear to me, that's how I learnt to reason, I use them all, all the words they showed me, there were columns of them, oh the strange glow all of a sudden, they were on lists with images opposite, I must have forgotten them, I must have mixed them up, these nameless images I have, these imageless names' (UN 407). Reason comes from mastering words in the vague recollection that they are founded on meanings that can no longer be remembered. Names deprived of images name only themselves; a confession deprived of the first sin reenancts only the form of sinning, continually reasserting the 'I' that thinks, the 'I' that sins.

By the time one is aware of listening, the steady whisper of 'I' that the others have spoken has set the stage of desire. That is, one begins to long for a self by the time he knows himself as one who listens, so that the speaker is literally born of the others' words. The speaker can say this at times: 'the words are everywhere, inside me, outside me, well well, a minute ago I had no thickness, I hear them, no need to hear them . . . I'm in words, made of words, others' words' (UN 386). But this awareness does not give him what he seeks: 'they say I seek what it is I hear' (UN 387). He seeks his 'I' that is made of others' words, seeks himself in another's representation. Because a self cannot be sensed immediately, the speaker is left in the situation of being unable to distinguish the 'I' he speaks from the 'I' he hears. This division produces the lack that propels desire. 'Let me now sum up, after this digression, there is I, I feel it, I confess, I give in, there is I, it's essential . . . there is I on the one hand, and this noise on the other' (UN 388). Of course one *feels* it; and one confesses in order to drag another in. For feeling is eternally enslaved to its betrayer, language, and language works feelingly only with the complicity of another.

The confessional dialogue hangs on this paradoxical use of language. Each discourse contains its own intentions and demands lip service to its ends: reason proposes to convey a truth just as confession proposes to reveal a sin. But the speaker's desire is elsewhere and can be followed only through a perversion of the discourse. Beckett had recognized that 'communication' cannot be a proper function of language as early as his *Proust*: 'Either we speak and act for ourselves – in which case speech and action are distorted and emptied of their meaning by an intelligence that is not ours, or we speak and act for others – in which case we speak and act a lie' (47). Although the young Beckett is arguing here for the necessary solitude of the writer who must speak only for himself, what he acknowledges is that either a listener will appropriate the speaker's language for his own purpose, or the speaker will 'lie' (be false to a *feeling* of one's true voice) to affect another. In both cases a listener is implied, though

121

only the latter fully acknowledges the bound conflict of the dialogic situation, to which *The Unnamable* with its explicitly master/servant relationship clearly belongs. Accordingly, the speaker in the book always speaks ostensibly to and for another (to them), though his desire is to speak of himself alone.

A passage about this confusion of pronouns suggests profound sources for the guilt aroused by this desire for a proper 'I.'

I seem to speak, that's because he says I as if he were I, I nearly believed him, do you hear him as if he were I, I who am far, who can't move, can't be found, but neither can he, he can only talk, if that much, perhaps it's not he, perhaps it's a multitude, one after another, what confusion, someone mentions confusion, is it a sin, all here is sin, you don't know why, you don't know whose, you don't know against whom, someone says you, it's the fault of the pronouns, there is no name for me, no pronoun for me.

(UN 403–4)

Because the speaker does not possess the 'I' as his own pronoun, he cannot identify himself in the discourse. In a discussion of personal pronouns, Benveniste makes the point that the pronoun 'I' has its reference only within a particular instance of discourse: 'I signifies "the person who is uttering the present instance of the discourse containing I" ' (Benveniste 218). In another essay he extends this point, noting that 'man constitutes himself as a *subject*' in language and establishes the concept of ' "ego" in reality': ' "Ego" is he who *says* "ego" ' (Benveniste 224). The saying of 'I' is sufficient to announce the concept of a subject, which is quickly reified by each into a self. But the speaker cannot claim possession of that self, or even of the subjectivity, though he now desires it. The speaker calls this gap between the 'I' and the desired self-presence sin. And if sin is a gap, then the closure of this gap in the ability to voice an authentic 'I am' would be equivalent to the sinless state of grace, to silence. Pronouns, that is, merely give expression to the desire for this state beyond speech.

The situation suggests a correspondence of the 'I' to the tetragrammaton, YHWH, a name so nearly consubstantial with the divine being that it was too sacred to be spoken. The Yahwist, in what is usually seen as a folk etymology[7] interprets the name as 'I am who I am' (Exodus 3.14). God is the sole 'I am,' the 'I' that 'before the sinning' would be the only one spoken. With the fall, with Satan's 'I am,' the confusion begins, and God's pronoun is veiled behind the

silence of ineffable YHWH.[8] But godhead lingers in the usurped
'I,' forever pointing to the difference between him who speaks the
pronoun and the divine being to whom it belongs. When *The Unnamable*'s speaker says 'I am,' he is mimicking the god-like authority
of them who gave him the words, as he simultaneously rejects them
by claiming his own godhead. Sin and grace are again joined in a
single movement of imitation and rivalry that infects every
statement.

The 'fault of the pronouns' is that they recall a fundamental will
to power involved in each act of speech. They play on the narcissism
of the listener, tempting him to hear in every phrase that is given to
him intimations of his own immortal 'I am.' The point when the
speaker awakens to the recognition of 'I' in his mouth does not,
however, mark the emergent sense of a self but of its loss: 'Where
now? Who now? When now? Unquestioning. I, say I. Unbelieving'
(UN 291, first page, first line). The totality that the infant's Ideal-I
had contained is fragmented by his saying 'I' into other places,
voices, and moments. The speaker says 'I' not believing in a self but
desiring it. Since he sees the self as a lack, it is the other that he
necessarily *believes* to be the site of being to which he turns for satisfaction. The speaker's narcissism does not display itself, therefore, in a
concentration of attention on the self – such simple enjoyments are
lost with infancy – but in the speaker's constitution of the other as
an autonomous being, as the possessor of the phallus, as the
castrator, as the extractor of obligations. Thus the speaker in *The Unnamable* addresses his speech to an other in his desire to possess that
supposed authority.

The text of *The Unnamable* is the speaker's attempt to represent
those prior others as the autonomous being he desires to be. Such
autonomy, however, does not exist. Those others, whether they are
other texts, fathers, teachers, or masters, have ultimate authority
only in the desiring eyes of the speaker, not in any real body less than
God's. Consequently, the speaker's representations will always fail to
achieve a representation perfectly consistent with any actual other. All
he can produce are versions of his imaginary ideal, each inadequate
because there is no ultimate signified to support it. But as the words
given to the speaker suggest to him the existence of some final presence,
the speaker's own attempts suggest the real existence of an author who
grounds the book, of an other the reader might eventually disclose

through interpretation. *The Unnamable*'s critics' naming the speaker 'the Unnamable,' as I show above, displays this desire to see a coherent subjectivity operating within the text so that the task of reading will produce a reflection worthy of their own labor. They find in Beckett's works that the difficulty, even impossibility, of telling a story makes Beckett's refusal to lapse into a despairing silence only further evidence of his heroic humanity, makes him the paragon of modernist man. Such readings relinquish their interpretive discourse to the appropriating power of the text; they take the confessor at his own word as one whose nobility is revealed only through his failings, his sins.

On the last pages of the text, this shift from the speaker to the reader as the interpreter and storyteller becomes explicit. The speaker increasingly uses the second person, implicating the reader in the project and transforming him into the next avatar of memory and obligation. He says of the repetitions that fill the text, 'the same words recur and they are your memories' (UN 395), which has by this time become literally true of the reader-as-'you.' The speaker's words are, in fact, part of the reader's memory. Very near the end he speaks of the way confession employs these memories:

I'll make myself a memory, I have only to listen, the voice will tell me everything, tell it to me again, everything I need, in dribs and drabs, breathless, it's like a confession, a last confession, you think it's finished, then it starts off again, there were so many sins, the memory is so bad, the words don't come, the words fail, the breath fails, no it's something else, it's an indictment, a dying voice accusing, accusing me.   (UN 411)

The speaker is proposing simply to listen, to open himself up as a vessel of memory where the confession of the other would have a place. That other confession would then *be* 'myself': the 'I' would become not the other but the simple remembering of a confession. By this point, the speaker no longer claims to be a listener, although he might make himself another's memory, yours. The speaker 'confesses' to the reader who always expects the tale to conclude ('You think it's finished'), who imagines that he will soon hold the speaker himself in his memory in a final, objectifed presence. The confusion of pronouns is no longer between 'I' and 'them' but 'I' and 'you': your memories are me.

But more significant is the shift that occurs when confession becomes accusation, for this shift explicitly involves the reader in the guilt that has motivated the entire discourse. Through confession, the guilt should end, but the reader discovers the guilt is his and his the obligation to take up the narrative. The guilt is always the same – the unlawful desire to possess the 'I' – and this is what the critic feels stirring in him with his attempts to objectify the voice of *The Unnamable*. In the last few lines of the book, the speaker feels 'they're going to abandon me,' which should imply the loss of his voice; but it is not the end. He says repeatedly, 'you must go on.'

You must go on, I can't go on, you must say words as long as there are any, until they find me, until they say me, strange pain, strange sin, you must go on.   (UN 414)

The next confession is beginning in these lines with the speaker adjuring his listener to continue and the listener (*The Unnamable*'s reader) already speaking the alluring 'I.' One 'I' going silent commanding another 'I' to 'find me . . . say me,' at which the listener awakens to a pain and sin that is still strange to him until he says, 'I'll go on.' The listener must recognize the sin as his and enter into the discourse of the text. The last words are: 'you must go on, I can't go on, I'll go on.' The pattern repeats the conclusion to *Molloy*: 'Then I went back into the house and wrote, It is midnight. The rain is beating on the windows. It was not midnight. It was not raining.' Two voices speak: past and present, writer and reader. The burden of speech that has tormented the speaker passes from them, the past, to whoever submits to reading the book. The reader has not been overhearing a confession, but has been a part of it.

IV

I have argued throughout this chapter that the critical readings of Beckett's work, of *The Unnamable* in particular, have consistently misread the texts in ways that produce illusions of real or potential authorial being with whom the readers could form a flattering identification. Such readings are included already in the text, though in parodistic, failed forms. The texts are not merely the stutterings of 'impotence,' a concept which, it should be clear by now, is the delusional consequence of a desire for potency; but neither are they evidence of Beckett's human triumph over meaninglessness. They are, rather, part of a compulsive process that informs all aspects of

125

desire, with this difference: they allow the reader to witness the form of his seduction, and perhaps to enter its exchange.

The text of *The Unnamable* works within a dualistic frame continually to stir up 'the two old maladies' Beckett refers to in 'Three Dialogues': 'wanting to know what to do and . . . wanting to be able to do it.' The maladies, importantly, are not an ignorance of what to do and an inability to do it, but the *wanting*. The impotence of Beckett's various speakers, far from being their problem, is their deluded triumph, the confirmation of a lost paradise. Consequently, any reading of *The Unnamable* that approaches the text as a 'journey into chaos' or an exploration of impotence and silence is already working within the maladies. To *exploit* impotence means something else. The confessional discourse of the text is not a remedy but might be considered a response to or acknowledgment of the maladies. Although this discourse too arouses desire, it consistently denies the reader any possibility of fulfillment. It reveals itself, rather, as the form of desire, which can duplicate itself in any context, infecting any structure with its hierarchical dualisms, planting the insidious pseudo-memory of bliss. In its manifestations, the form reproduces the various knots of conflict – between parent and child, God and man, confessor and confessor, writer and reader. Such conflicts can be interpreted only by a discourse that supplements it, continuing its form but displacing its terms, supplanting its authority; for these conflicts are fundamentally resistant to explanation. They exist within irreducible indeterminacies of language that continuously generate the oppositions they strive to overcome.

Lacan noted that there is 'aggressivity . . . in any relation to the other,' no matter how altruistic, because aggressivity focuses the force arising from the 'connection between the narcissistic libido and the alienation function of the "I" ' (*Écrits* 6). The fact of having to say 'I' means that the speaker will desire to appropriate the other as a necessary complement to his own being. Those philosophies he sees as 'directly issuing from the *Cogito*,' in which he includes the existentialist dualism of Being and Nothingness, are committed to the 'I' and thus to the mastery of the other. A reader working from within such a philosophy would have to read for the revelation of the 'I,' for the conclusion of the confession. *The Unnamable* develops not in the service of this narcissistic libido, but in a recognition of it. Lacan suggests a limit to his own dialogues that could also define a telos for the

Beckettian confession: to reach 'the ecstatic limit of the "Thou art that" ' (*Écrits* 7) where the ideal of the autonomous ego would be abandoned. But Lacan realizes that such an end is outside the analytic dialogue, is outside language, and hence outside the knowable, for our way of knowing is the rational. Derrida makes a similar point about such limits: 'The unsurpassable, unique, and imperial grandeur of the order of reason, that which makes it not just another actual order or structure . . . is that one cannot speak out against it except by being for it, that one can protest it only from within it' ('Cogito' 36). Beckett's speaker displays this limit with every longing for silence, as do Beckett's critics who laud him as the master of the discourse of silence. The difference is that Beckett's critics tend to see the continual assaults on the limit as man's triumph against futility, the power of creativity over nothingness, while Beckett's text confesses to its motivations in the narcissistic aggression of impotence.

The reader who desires the escape from language into silence will be the victim of another who has discovered, consciously or not, that language is the instrument of power, not truth. He will submit himself to any tormentor, avenging God, or threatening father so long as the suffering and obligation incurred can be given a meaning. To read *The Unnamable* as if it were narrated from a single ego, the Unnamable, is to turn to Beckett as the castrator-comforter who allows the reader to be impotent rather than alone.[9] Beckett neither escapes the dilemma – its foundations are too firmly embedded in the language – nor offers the reader release. But he does offer a text that, if one accepts its implications, allows the reader to see that every pose of impotence is merely the veil for an impudent will to power. Punishment (like penance) is also crime; representation is the dangerous supplement; writing is appropriation: all are motivated by a desire for a bliss that is irrecoverably lost. In the compulsive confession of *The Unnamable* is the possibility for a reader to be conscious of his motivations in the midst of his complicity in the act, to know that although we are made of others' words, we go on through the desire to master the language of all others.

6
Conclusion

The web

The gift of a well-told tale is one few would want to refuse, but to accept can imply obligations and complicities that are hard to escape. The seriousness of this complicity, for both teller and listener, is one of the themes of Manuel Puig's *The Kiss of the Spider Woman*. The story involves two men sharing a jail cell in a repressive state. Molina, a homosexual arrested on morals charges, tells Valentin, a middle-class intellectual turned revolutionary, the plots of old movies to pass the time. For Valentin, the stories are a break in his discipline of political study, a program he finds necessary to maintain his commitment to the cause since being separated from his comrades. But even during these entertainments, he subjects Molina's tales to rigorous psychoanalytic and Marxist analyses and is intolerant of Molina's corruptions of the original movie plots and his unwillingness to think about the implications of his stories. 'Don't waste so much time, tell me what happens' (SW 50), Valentin protests when Molina begins to fill his stories with details irrelevant to the plot. But for Molina, apparently, the plot is less important than the surface texture of the story, its atmosphere, its power of evocation.

Molina's indirection and elaboration are implicitly dangerous to Valentin's discipline: Valentin cannot afford to forget that his life is bound up with the goals of a class of people. Listening to the story of a movie made by the Nazis in which the members of the French resistance are the villains, he protests:

—Do you know what the maquis were?
—Yes, I already know they were patriotic, but in this film they're not. Let me finish, okay? So . . . let's see, what happened next?
—I don't understand you at all.
—Well, it's just that the film was divine, and for me that's what counts, because I'm locked up in this cell and I'm better off thinking about nice things, so I don't go nuts, see? . . . Well?
—What do you want me to say?
—That you'll let me escape from reality once in a while, because why should I let myself get more depressed than I am? (SW 78)

Molina's formalism, his unwillingness to see that the story is part of a larger reality, offends Valentin. Molina, on the other hand, claims 'art' as a realm where the horror and absurdity of life can be denied despite the conscious knowledge of its artificiality. The argument is an old one, and because it is so old, so common, we fail to realize for a long time that it is a ruse. Molina, it turns out, has been placed in the cell to win the confidence of the revolutionary and betray him to the police. He is to seduce Valentin.

Ultimately, it is the stories that seduce Valentin with their formal coherence. In his desire to understand the stories intellectually, he becomes involved with the telling, gradually coming to share the discourse that defines Molina. And as he comes to share it, empathy, an intersubjective knowing, replaces rationality, as repetition replaces analysis. As he adopts Molina's narrative style, Valentin begins to interpret himself through a discourse almost identical to that of Molina. As a consequence, he comes to 'understand,' even to love Molina, although this means, in fact, that he is at Molina's mercy, just as the police had intended. The police, it would seem, are the only ones in control. But the dynamics of the confessional dialogue are not finally subject to a single intention, either Molina's or the police's. The mastery Molina achieves has its own demands that the police cannot satisfy, so he cannot directly betray his victim. As he invests his stories in Valentin, he becomes dependent on Valentin to represent him, to continue his discourse. He needs to preserve Valentin as his memory and avatar, safe from the reduction to the literalness of the police language. For both of the prisoners, the desire to establish some control over their world – through art or through rationality – leads them into a conspiracy of narration and interpretation that binds them together. We could call that bind love, but we should recognize that it is born out of a struggle to appropriate the other, a struggle that ultimately serves the ends of the police regardless of anyone's intention.

The story provides a way of undertstanding the claims of many twentieth-century writers and their critics that the writer's art is the individual genius's refusal to accept that 'the end of life is lying still,' as Faulkner and Minter put it. Such claims, like Hawthorne's vague 'moral blossom,' are for all their nobility deeply dissatisfying. I say this not because I doubt these writers' integrity or suspect them of hypocrisy. Rather, the claims, if we extend them to other great writers, assume that writers, almost uniquely among mankind, are willing to dedicate themselves to lives of self-conscious futility. It is the kind of assumption that generates flatteringly contradictory descriptions of the project of writing: the failures are splended, the impotent are grand, the sinners are righteous. All such formulations arise from the gap that appears between the writer's intention and the promise of a conclusion. Between its source in authorial intention and its completion in unrealized perfection, success is defined by failure, for without these two impossibilities of origin and end, not only do categories such as failure and impotence have no meaning, but the very idea of the writer's greatness comes into question.

It is not hard to understand why we would wish to retain these categories, for through them we take comfort in what we otherwise do not understand by preserving the human and moral dimension that a controlling author can provide. Nietzsche argues in *Beyond Good and Evil* that value in language is grounded in the intention of the writer. Intention is held to be the evidence of the individual living in the words: it provides the man behind the stories whom Valentin comes to love. But as Nietzsche also points out, the practice of reasoning from cause to effect (from intention to work) is almost always a delusion, a rationalization to justify the effects we have produced: intention is never more than the belated supposition we impose on a work. All that can be known for certain is the effect we see in the world, not the causes. A Nietzschean reasoning, like Freud's, assumes there are no accidents, but the effect may be the manifestation of an intention that the agent neither knows of nor is able to control. The value of a work and the greatness of a writer become problematic when the work of production is seen as occurring through the agency of forces that have their own ends. The police saw that they did not need Molina's conscious cooperation to achieve their ends because Molina was already complicit in a structure of power and sexuality over which he had no control. He seduces Valentin without any intent to do so, just as he comes to depend on Valentin despite intending not to.

I would not want to reduce Hawthorne, Beckett, and Faulkner to versions of Molina. Rather, I have attempted to release them from the resolute denial of those who, like Molina, will not see what these writers are doing lest they be forced to recognize their own complicity in the dialogue. Unlike Molina, the writers I have discussed seem, in their works at least, not only to be aware of this dynamic, but to display it for their readers. It is the pattern of seduction, appropriation, and repetition that forms the web of their books and that I have pointed to as the demonstration and revelation of a narrative power.

In each case, the power of the speaker to engage a listener in the confessional dialogue depends on the ability to find the interpretive structure the reader will most readily adopt. Such structures are often taken as 'natural,' which means only that the knowledge produced by them is positive, the guaranteed outcome of a completed interpretive task. In Hawthorne's narrative, for instance, Dimmesdale's ability to seduce his audience, to inspire a passion in them compounding religious and romantic ecstasy, depends on his speaking from within a powerful and well-defined discourse of Puritanism. That discourse seems to guarantee for them the ultimate interpretability of his confessional sermons despite their evasiveness. The parishioners can abandon themselves to the sermons, confident that the words will lead them back to the bosom of the church. But the mystery at the center of Dimmesdale's sermons is less a matter of the unfathomable depths of the divine than of the implicit gap between any signifying form and an ultimate truth toward which it is directed. It is a gap that the wholly righteous, if there were such, would never discover, for a subjectivity formed by the language of righteousness would experience reality in full accord with the language available to represent it. World and meaning would be knit into a seamless whole. But the sinners who are his audience feel the gap between themselves and God, between their language and His Word. Dimmesdale discovers that what language can express is the 'truth' of that gap, of the failure of language to serve its revelatory function, a failure analogous to the 'failure' of Christians to become Christ.

And yet the message the parishioners hear is not one of despair but of hope, because Dimmesdale, the apparent source of this wisdom, seems not to suffer this separation from God that the rest of them do. Because his confessions point so clearly to the loss each feels, his common words seem to contain the promise of a full speech, with every word adequate to its transcendent meaning. Given the tremendous power and prestige Dimmesdale achieves by exploiting the language of transgression, the fact that he continues to speak despite the 'failure' implicit in his language is hardly a testament to his courage, spirit, or nobility. He not only derives great rewards from his position, which would be reason enough to continue; he also becomes increasingly dependent on the response he elicits from his listeners, needing the confirmation they provide for his own sense of who he is. Having lost any spiritual centeredness that he may have felt when living a more perfect imitation of Christ, he knows himself only as he is represented in the adulation and imitation of his listeners; he *is* what is represented by his discourse, and he is thereby bound to those who can hear and repeat him.

This brief summary of Dimmesdale's position in the novel cannot do justice to the elaboration of this pattern in the work as a whole. It does not, for example, touch the challenge that Hester's own appropriation of the Puritan community's signs, and of Dimmesdale's own language, presents to Dimmesdale's authority. And it can only anticipate the similar pattern of seduction and obligation that the narrator of the Custom House develops with his readers through the interpretive structures of the Romance. But it displays how, for the religious parishioner, as for the 'Romance' reader, the threads of his 'natural' discourse are the nearly invisible constituents of a promising web of meaning: the language itself is what is not noticed, because to notice it is to acknowledge its source in the conventions of an arbitrary structure and its lack of any absolute meaning.

The patterns of repetition and obligation become more visible when compared to similar patterns in the other books. In both *The Unnamable* and *Absalom, Absalom!*, powerful institutional models are invoked that determine the initial possibilities for understanding. Although the speaker of *The Unnamble* is cut off from almost all knowledge of the world through his senses, he never abandons the idea that there are things about which he can obtain some positive knowledge: about himself, for instance, or 'them,' his tormentors, masters, and predecessors. His assumption that such a knowledge is possible derives from a faith in a dualistic ordering of the world which he projects onto a metaphysical realm: effects must have causes, words must have referents, speakers must have intentions, thinking must have an 'I' that thinks. When this structure is projected onto a metaphysical plane, it is no longer just the convenient hermeneutic of a Cartesian dualism but the guarantee that ultimate causes, intentions, meanings and subjective beings exist and can be found. Like Dimmesdale's parishioners, the speaker can give himself over to the language 'they' have provided, thinking that if he can just go on long enough, the words will release him from his obligations.

132

But this account is not quite fair to the speaker, who is not finally at all confident that his task will actually end. Neither, however, does he seem to be Georges Duthuit's hero who makes the impossibility of meaning his meaning. As becomes clear by the end of the Trilogy, the obligation to understand is not the burden solely of the speaker in relation to the 'them' who preceded him. It has been shifted to the reader, to 'You' who must go on, carrying on (as so many writers have done after Beckett) the endless play of a discourse that seems to pursue what cannot be found. For most readers and critics, of course, it is not this 'speaker' but Beckett, the enigmatic genius behind the text, who is pursued: despite the evident hollowness of the Beckettian subject, the web of the Beckettian text must, they assume, contain its priceless reward, the master himself. It would be too cruel to conclude that the text is part of a seduction, that its effect is not to reveal the authorial consciousness but to oblige subsequent readers to attempt to represent the writer. Beckett's seeming awareness of this aspect of writing does not lead him to escape it; rather, he draws attention to the lines of the text, to the web that otherwise remains concealed as a second nature.

The failure to escape this Natural perspective, or even to recognize its existence, drives the characters of *Absalom, Absalom!* toward their appalling, tragic ends. The genetic accidents that have produced the distinctions we call 'race' have become linked to purely social conventions of class and family, which have transformed skin color into meaning, mere physical traits into metaphysical qualities. The idea of a white race depends on a myth of original purity, supported by some absolute blankness contained in the womb of a virgin. If one is white, all ancestors back to the origin must be white. But this requirement means no one can know exactly who he is since the origin cannot be known. The origin is not just a place from which one begins, but the truth of the family and the individual. And since all origins are suspect, the lives of the characters of *Absalom, Absalom!* are consumed by the attempt to repress the recognition that all family lines are eventually corrupt and to create a narrative that can stand in its place. In the impossibility of becoming the literal 'father-head' of a family, each teller of the tale of Sutpen tries to become the story-head, the one whom all subsequent tellers will attempt to explain and complete. The various fictions of family, race, class, virginity, and miscegenation are the invisible, because 'natural,' threads of culture from which each of the narrators chooses to assemble his or her tale. The effect of the stories is to repress the fact that these categories are not natural, and thereby to repress also the realization that they will never provide a final conclusion to the story. Like the other narrators I have discussed, those of *Absalom, Absalom!* remain unaware of their purposes, the repression of their narrative working its effect on them as well as their listeners. All narrators struggle to master history, to discover the truth of their origins and thereby escape the domination of the past. And because they focus on this impossible task, they are never forced to realize that they are in fact working to dominate their listeners. The actual expression of a will to power is not toward the past, but to the future that will take place within the discourse already created by a powerful narrator, but a discourse that is already entangled in the resentment of a past narrator. Sutpen never escaped the tales of race, Haitian success, and dynasty he learned as a child, but he was able to appropriate enough of the power of those tales to inflict them on subsequent generations of listeners. *Absalom, Absalom!*'s storyteller's comfort, his revenge, his triumph is not that he escapes the web of the past, but that he obligates others to work with his version of it. In the failure to recognize, or the fear of acknowledging, the conventional nature of what they are engaged in, the narrators of *Absalom, Absalom!* compulsively repeat patterns of obligation and desire that destroy themselves and those around them.

The power of this pattern to perpetuate itself depends on the desire of readers and writers for mastery; not necessarily that they will be masters, but that someone will be. This is not mastery in the sense of greatness: Beckett is a greater writer. Mastery, as I have been using the word, implies being in control of one's meanings, finding a discourse adequate to one's intentions. The master is able to control his and others' representation, which means he controls the constitutive forms of reality. Mastery, therefore, is always a form of domination, but since it means that someone, sometimes knows what he is doing, it is one few would be willing to abandon.

To resist mastery, it is not enough to claim that no one is a master: this is the position of the clown, the impotent, the magnificent failure, as well as the devout priest acknowledging the incomprehensibility of the divine Word. Such a position denies the possibility of attaining any absolute knowledge, but it tacitly accepts the discourse of the absent master. Vereker's critic undermines the writer's mastery of his novels in 'The Figure in the Carpet,' just as we might see Quentin undermining the myths of race and class in his South or Dimmesdale undermining the theocractic domination of Boston. But in each case they do so only to perpetuate a discourse, thereby extending the real dominion of a force that determines the way others will represent, and therein know, their world. The complicity they show with those who tell them their stories has ultimately little to do with a desire to further the particular interests of the tellers, but with the willingness the listeners show to accept the terms of mastery embodied in the discourses they share.

The implications of the argument here go beyond the limits of a literary study. Because social and political lives are built around the stories a people hear and tell each other, the question of discourse and mastery touches on the possibility of knowing how one is placed in the world. The alternative is not to adopt a discourse free of the intimations of mastery, for no such discourse exists in our culture. But what is possible is an analytic that does not accept the offer to follow out the story one is told, to listen to the confession, and to understand it. Any pursuit of a positive knowledge in the imitation of a science will produce the complicity that elevates the arbitrary to the transcendent. An analytic that turns away from knowing and looks at the sources of knowledge in the discourses constructed by culture will not enable one to escape those sources into some mythic existential freedom. It may, however, enable one to avoid the compulsive, and often destructive, pursuit of masters and mastery that is no less mythic. And recognizing that the confessional dialogue is built not on sin but within a web of language, teller and listener might even forgo the pleasures of seduction to engage the complexities of the web itself.

Notes

Chapter 1. The confessional turn

[1] François Roustang argues that very serious threats to Freud's mastery were presented by several of his disciples. What was particularly dangerous to their positions was that they could not be countered or incorporated by Freud's rationality. They each offered a language of psychoanalysis, not a problem, and therefore challenged Freud not as neurosis but as psychosis, not as a father's name but as a mother's tongue. Such differences are outside the realm of what I call confession.

[2] I do not take up the vast possibilities of explicitly confessional works such as Rousseau's or de Quincey's, not because they would not be open to such interpretation but, in part, so that I will not seem to be limited to that particular genre.

[3] Louis Althusser provides a powerful analysis of the role played by the languages of family and church, among other institutions, in the production of subjects suited to the state's needs. In this analysis, it is ideology, not any consciously acquired meanings, that is conveyed by the forms of institutions and that shapes the individual. Confession, I am arguing, is powerfully ideological in these terms.

Chapter 2. Three exemplary readings

[1] See the chapter on Beckett's *The Unnamable* below for a discussion of a similar pattern in a post-Christian era.

[2] A good example is Robert Scholes's and Robert Kellogg's, *The Nature of Narrative* (215).

[3] This is something we shall see again in Faulkner's *Absalom! Absalom!*, where Sutpen's initial confession receives a series of readings within the text.

[4] Although a part of *Either/Or*, I will be limiting my discussion to this separately published text.

Chapter 3. The embroidered sin

[1] Feidelson suggests here that the Puritan's thinking was limited by having 'lost the capacity for symbolic thinking' (96) and thus for understanding logically nonsensical ideas (e.g. the Trinity). I would argue that the Puritan refusal of 'symbolic' thought in Feidelson's sense is the source of their vitality and of at least Dimmesdale's power. The task of understanding was always renewed and always inconclusive.

2 In 'Footsteps of Ann Hutchinson,' Michael Colacurcio establishes Hawthorne's concern with antinomianism in *The Scarlet Letter*.

3 In his 'Preface to Transgression,' Michel Foucault speaks of trangression's opening an 'affirmed world': 'It is the solar inversion of Satanic denial' (37). That is, trangression restores the solar center to the divine system that Satan had attempted to disperse among the scattered worlds of self-created gods. The risk that Satan took in denying God had at the very least the appeal of certainty: sin seems to promise either the self-presence reserved for the gods or the affirmation of God's presence through His retribution. The impossibility of knowing God absolutely, coupled with the constant desire to know, leads inevitably to transgression. The charm of doing wrong and the desire for the forbidden both result from a need to discover what one *is* without mediation. Transcendence or punishment: either would be an acceptable conclusion to sin.

4 Ernest W. Baughman makes it clear that private confession has no place in Puritan society. The act testified to the importance Puritans placed in one's association within a community.

5 The embroidery resembles here the subversion of what Derrida calls the 'supplement.' His essay, 'The Parergon,' is also relevant here in showing the possibility for a 'frame' to alter, even to displace the meaning of the framed.

6 Freud's discussion of symptoms is instructive here. That which originally protects one from the forbidden act comes to represent the act, providing both satisfaction and new sources of guilt (Freud, 'Repression' 111).

7 Kenneth Dauber's excellent discussion of Hawthorne's use of such disruptions of convention is weakened by his claim that these disruptions represent some authentic Hawthorne. John Franzosa's more penetrating insight – that 'if there is finally any referent for ["Rappaccini's Daughter"] it is Hawthorne's concern with the nature of his own authority as a writer' – recognizes the hopelessness of this concern: there is no nature behind the text ('Inflation' 13).

8 Daniel Cottom finds that Hawthorne's artful evasions provide a privileged realm of communication outside the physical imperatives of the world. This formulation seems to overlook the place of desire and the will to power in such evasive language. Hawthorne in the 'Custom House' resembles Dimmesdale in such use of evasion.

9 I use the term as developed by Girard in *Violence and the Sacred*, especially chapter 2.

10 Frequent mention of Hawthorne's intense desire to be read appears in Arlin Turner's recent biography.

Chapter 4. Love's androgynous advocates

1 Sundquist, for instance, argues at length that the constant threat of miscegenation is *the* flaw. It is a problem that Sundquist finds not just in the book, but in a reflection of the American South.

[2] Bleikasten borrows from Beckett's notion of 'impotence' in his conception of failure. In doing so, he reads Faulkner in an existentialist tradition of redemption through the acceptance of absurdity. See my following chapter on Beckett for an analysis of Beckettian impotence.

[3] See, for example, the essays by Estella Schoenberg and Susan Resneck Parr.

[4] Kenneth Burke has written of the narcissism of incest as it appears in the symbolic realm:

> Symbolic incest is often but a roundabout mode of self-engrossment, a narcissistic independence, quite likely at the decadent end of individualism, where the poet is but expressing in sexual imagery a pattern of thought that we might call simply 'communion with the self,' and is giving this state of mind concrete material body in the imagery of sexual cohabitation with someone 'of the same substance' as the self. (42)

Henry' poetic mediation between Bon and Judith is just such a symbolic incest, coming at that 'decadent end' where the individual has become equivalent to the Family House. An illustrative comparison would be Poe's House of Usher, wherein the identification of the individual and the house became inseparable from the incestuous involvement of Roderick and Madeline.

[5] John Irwin has established the legitimacy of reading *Absalom, Absalom!* in the context of Faulkner's other novels. Irwin suggests that Quentin hears Sutpen's story through his own preoccupation with incest as a means to revenge himself against his always-belated position in time. Mr Compson's decision to emphasize the aspects of incest in the story ensure his having an interested audience. Irwin also argues that Faulkner's own writing follows the same pattern of doubling and repetition that compels Quentin, an argument that has influenced much of my own thinking about Faulkner. But where Irwin's argument focuses on revenge as the attempt to close the Oedipal circle and defeat time, I emphasize the means by which revenge functions through a projection into the future. Before Quentin begins his own revision of Sutpen's life, he is already the victim of his father who has enlisted Quentin's desires and anxieties in an obligation to interpret. Quentin's revenge comes only when he can talk to Shreve.

[6] The issue appears in the first essay of *Écrits*, 'The Mirror Stage,' in the discussion of the symbolic stage. See also the final essay, 'The Subversion of the Subject and the Dialectic of Desire.'

[7] I take the association between the literary and modernity from Jacques Derrida's discussion in *Of Grammatology* (59). Modernity as an ahistorical impulse is also a central feature of Paul de Man's argument in the essay 'Literary History and Literary Modernity' (148).

[8] Freud writes in his essay 'Negation,' 'A negative judgment is the intellectual substitute for repression; the "no" in which it is expressed is the hallmark of repression, a certificate of origin, as it were, like "Made in Germany" ' (214). Repression is often the only origin we can identify.

Chapter 5. All here is sin

1 See for example, Robert Champigny's 'Adventures of the first Person.'

2 Federman, for example, says that each of Beckett's works is 'a critical reflection on previous achievements,' clinging to the idea of Beckett's work being successful (*Journey into Chaos* 16).

3 See, for example, Holland's 'Transactive Criticism: Re-creation Through Identity,' 'A Transactive Account of Transactive Criticism,' and Iser's *The Act of Reading* (9).

4 Sylvie Deberec Henning has written on this topic using a Heideggerian concept of 'stiving' toward a concealed truth. She posits that the difference between the writer and the double produced in the text leads to an endless pursuit. This use of 'striving' leads her to see the process as the 'veiling' of a truth that is, in the cliché, revealed because concealed. The result is that she relates the compulsion of writing to creativity and truth, concepts that recall the problems of a romantic existentialism.

5 Barthes makes a similar claim about 'criticism' that 'always deals with the texts of pleasure, never the texts of bliss.' Criticism, that is, is satisfied with ends that can be fully possessed (*Pleasure* 21).

6 Derrida has called this attempt to purge language a 'white mythology': a 'metaphysics which has effaced in itself that fabulous scene which brought it into being, and yet which remains, active and stirring' ('White Mythology' 11).

7 See, for example, The Cambridge Bible Commentary edition of *Exodus* (23).

8 According to the *American Heritage Dictionary of the English Language*, the verb 'to be' has several Indo-European roots. 'Am' derives from 'es,' which is also the root for 'sin': 'suffixed (collective) zero-grade from *sat-ia*, "that which is," in Germanic *sun(d)jo*, sin (<"it is true," "the sin is real"), in Old English synn, sin' (1515). The implication is that sin is related to an idea of being and, more curiously (if more distantly), to the expression of self-being, I am. Satan's sin, then, could be seen as his literally daring to say 'I am,' to declare his own existence.

9 Nietzsche does, however, extract an ambiguous virtue from such a willed impotence. It is, he claims, 'a will to nothingness' that 'despite everything . . . remains a *will* . . .: man would sooner have the void for his purpose than be void of purpose' (Nietzsche 298–9). The problems arise from man's refusal to face such a will as being basic to his motivations.

Works cited

Althusser, Louis. 'Ideology and Ideological State Apparatuses'. *Lenin and Philosophy*. Ben Brewster. New York: Monthly Review Press, 1971.

The American Heritage Dictionary of the English Language. Ed. William Morris. 1975.

Augustine. *Confessions*. Trans. R. S. Pine-Coffin. Middlesex, England: Penguin Books, 1961.

Barthes, Roland. *The Pleasure of the Text*. Trans. Richard Miller. New York: Hill and Wang-Farrar, Straus and Giroux, 1975.

Baughman, Ernest W. 'Public Confession in *The Scarlet Letter*.' *The New England Quarterly*, 40 (1967), 532–50.

Beckett, Samuel. *Proust*. New York: Grove Press, 1931.

　The Unnamable in *Three Novels by Samuel Beckett*. New York: Evergreen–Grove Press, 1965.

Benveniste, Emil. *Problems in General Linguistics*. Trans. Mary Elizabeth Meek. Coral Gables, Florida: University of Miami Press, 1971.

Bercovitch, Sacvan. *The American Jeremiad*. Madison, Wisconsin: University of Wisconsin Press, 1978.

　The Puritan Origins of the American Self. New Haven: Yale University Press, 1975.

Bishop, Tom and Federman, Raymond. *Samuel Beckett*. Paris: Éditions de l'Herne, 1976.

Bleikasten, Andre. *The Most Splendid Failure: Faulkner's 'The Sound and the Fury.'* Bloomington: Indiana University Press, 1976.

Brooks, Cleanth. *William Faulkner: The Yoknapatawpha Country*. New Haven: Yale University Press, 1963.

Brooks, Peter. 'Freud's Masterplot: Questions of Narrative.' *Yale French Studies* 55–6 (1977).

Burke, Kenneth. *The Philosophy of Literary Form*. Berkeley: University of California Press, 1973.

Champigny, Robert. 'Adventures of the First Person.' *Samuel Beckett Now*. Ed. Melvin J. Friedman. Chicago, Ill.: University of Chicago Press, 1970.

Cottom, Daniel. 'Hawthorne versus Hester: The Ghostly Dialectic of Romance in *The Scarlet Letter*.' *TSLL*, 24 (1982).

Crews, Frederick C. *The Sins of the Fathers: Hawthorne's Psychological Themes*. Madison Wisconsin: University of Wisconsin Press, 1978.

Dauber, Kenneth. *Rediscovering Hawthorne*. Princeton, N.J.: Princeton University Press, 1977.

Works cited

De Man, Paul. *Blindness and Insight: Essay in the Rhetoric of Contemporary Criticism*. 2nd Ed. Minneapolis: University of Minnesota Press, 1983.

Derrida, Jacques. 'Differance.' *Speech and Phenomena: And Other Essays on Husserl's Theory of Signs*. Trans. David B. Allison. Evanston, Ill.: Northwestern University Press, 1973.

Of Grammatology. Trans. Gayatri Chakravorty Spivak. Baltimore: The Johns Hopkins University Press, 1974.

'White Mythology.' *NLH* 6 (1974), 5–74.

Writing and Difference. Trans. Alan Bass. Chicago, Ill.: University of Chicago Press, 1978.

Dryden, Edgar A. *Nathaniel Hawthorne: The Poetics of Enchantment*. Ithaca: Cornell University Press, 1977.

Exodus. The Cambridge Bible Commentary. Ed. Comm. Ronald E. Clements. Cambridge, England: The Cambridge University Press, 1972.

Faulkner, William. *Absalom, Absalom!*. New York: Modern Library–Random House, 1936.

Federman, Raymond. *Journey into Chaos*. Berkeley, Calif.: University of California Press, 1965.

Feidelson, Charles, Jr. *Symbolism and American Literature*. Chicago: University of Chicago Press, 1953.

Foucault, Michel. *The Archaeology of Knowledge*. Trans. A. M. Sheridan Smith. New York: Harper Torchbooks–Harper and Row, 1972.

The Order of Things: An Archaeology of the Human Sciences, New York: Vintage, 1973.

Language, Counter-Memory, Practice. Ithaca, N.Y.: Cornell University Press, 1977.

Franzosa, John. 'The Language of Inflation in "Rappaccini's Daughter." ' *TSLL*, 24 (1982).

Freccero, John. 'The Fig Tree and the Laurel: Petrarch's Poetics.' *Diacritics* 5 (1975).

Freud, Sigmund. 'The "Uncanny." ' Trans. Alex Strachey. *On Creativity and the Unconscious: Papers on the Psychology of Art, Literature, Love, Religion*. Ed. Benjamin Nelson. New York: Harper Colophon Books–Harper and Row, 1958.

Beyond the Pleasure Principle. Trans. and Ed. James Strachey. Standard Edition 18, 1955. Rpt. New York: W. W. Norton & Co., 1961.

Civilization and Its Discontents. Trans. James Strachey. New York: W. W. Norton and Co., 1961.

'Negation.' *General Psychological Theory: Papers on Metapsychology*. Ed. Philip Rieff. Trans. Joan Riviere. New York: Collier–Macmillan, 1963.

'Psychoanalytic Notes Upon an Autobiographical Account of a Case of Paranoia' (The Psychotic Dr Schreber). *Three Case Histories*. Ed. Philip Rieff. New York: Collier Books–Macmillan Publishing Co., 1963.

'Repression.' Trans. Cecil M. Baines. *General Psychological Theory*. New York: Collier, 1963.

141

Works cited

Girard, René. *Violence and the Sacred*. Trans. Patrick Gregory. Baltimore, Md.: The Johns Hopkins University Press, 1977.

Hawthorne, Nathaniel. *The Scarlet Letter*. Norton Critical Edition, 2nd ed. Eds. Sculley Bradley et al. New York: W. W. Norton, 1978.

Hegel, George Wilhelm Friedrich. *Phenomenology of Spirit*. Trans. A. V. Miller. New York: Oxford University Press, 1977.

Henning, Sylvie Deberec. 'Narrative and Textual Doubles in the Works of Samuel Beckett.' *Sub-Stance* 29 (1981), 97–105.

Holland, Norman. 'A Transactive Account of Transactive Criticism.' *Poetics* 7 (1978), 177–89.

'Transactive Criticism: Re-creation Through Identity.' *Criticism* 18 (1976), 334–52.

Howe, Irving. *William Faulkner: A Critical Study*. Chicago: University of Chicago Press, 1975.

Iser, Wolfgang. *The Act of Reading: A Theory of Aesthetic Response*. Baltimore, Md.: The Johns Hopkins University Press, 1978.

Irwin, John T. *Doubling and Incest/Repetition and Revenge*. Baltimore: The Johns Hopkins University Press, 1975.

James, Henry. 'The Figure in the Carpet.' *Eight Tales from the Major Phase*. Ed. Morton Daumer Zabel. New York: W. W. Norton and Co., 1958.

Kartiganer, Donald M. *The Fragile Thread: The Meaning of Form in Faulkner's Novels*. Amherst: The University of Massachusetts Press, 1979.

Kenner, Hugh. *Samuel Beckett*. Berkeley, Calif.: University of California Press, 1961.

Kierkegaard, Soren. *Diary of a Seducer*. Trans. Gerd Gillhoff. New York: Frederick Ungar Publishing Co., 1966.

Lacan, Jacques. *'Écrits: A Selection*. Trans. Alan Sheridan. London: Tavistock Publications Limited, 1977.

Lawrence, D. H. *Studies in Classic American Literature*. Garden City, N.Y.: Doubleday, 1951.

McConnell, Frank D. *The Confessional Imagination: A Reading of Wordsworth's 'Prelude.'* Baltimore, Md.: The Johns Hopkins University Press, 1974.

Minter, David. *William Faulkner: His Life and Works*. Baltimore, Md.: The Johns Hopkins University Press, 1980.

Nietzsche, Friedrich. *The Birth of Tragedy* and *The Genealogy of Morals*. Trans. Francis Golffing. Garden City, New York: Anchor–Doubleday, 1956.

Parr, Susan Resneck. 'The Fourteenth Image of the Blackbird: Another Look at Truth in *Absalom, Absalom!*' *Arizona Quarterly* 35 (1979), 153–64.

Puig, Manuel. *The Kiss of the Spider Woman*. Trans. Thomas Colchie. New York: Knopf, 1979.

Ricoeur, Paul. *The Symbolism of Evil*. Trans. Emerson Buchanan. New York: Harper and Row, 1967.

Roustang, François. *Dire Mastery: Discipleship From Freud to Lacan*. Trans. Ned Lukacher, Baltimore: Johns Hopkins, 1982.

Rowe, John Carlos. 'The Internal Conflict of Romantic Narrative: Hegel's *Phenomenology* and Hawthorne's *The Scarlet Letter*.' *MLN* 95 (1980), 1203–31.

Works cited

Schoenberg, Estella. *Old Tales and Talking: Quentin Compson in William Faulkner's 'Absalom, Absalom!' and Related Works*. Jackson, Miss.: University Press of Mississippi, 1977.

Scholes, Robert and Robert Kellogg. *The Nature of Narrative*. New York: Oxford University Press, 1966.

Shenker, Israel. 'Moody Man of Letters.' *New York Times*, May 6, 1956, sec. 2, p. 3.

Stoever, William K. *'A Faire and Easie Way to Heaven': Covenant Theology and Antinomianism in Early Massachusetts*. Middletown, Conn.: Wesleyan University Press, 1978.

Tobin, Patricia Drechsel. *Time and the Novel: The Genealogical Imperative*. Princeton; Princeton University Press, 1978.

Turner, Arlin. *Nathaniel Hawthorne: A Biography*. New York: Oxford University Press, 1980.

Index

allegory, 47
Althusser, Louis, 136n4
appropriation: of discourses, 28, 33, 40, 48, 58; as mastery, 41, 42, 79, 81; by servant, 119

Barthes, Roland, 112–13
Benveniste, Emile, 122
Burke, Kenneth, 138n4

communication: as a model, 2, 12, 52; and Reader Response, 41; as sin, 55
conventionality: of authority, 82; of confession, 4; of criticism, 46–7; of family, 79, 86; of history, 85, 92, 94; of love, 30, 32; of race, 101–2; of reason, 120, 127; repression of c., 104; of Romance, 73–4; of sin, 3, 15, 23, 54, 58, 65

Dante, 119
Derrida, Jacques, 10, 56, 111, 127, 137n5
double bind, 78

first person [see also 'subject'], 3, 10: as 'eye,' 44–5; as YHWH, 122; as subject, 105–7; in Lacan, 110, 117, 122, 123; as 'you,' 124, 133
Foucault, Michel, 13–14, 60, 82, 137n3
Freccero, John, 26
Freud, Sigmund, 5–6, 7, 13, 138n8

Hegel, G. W. F., 4, 5, 13

impotence, 41, 130: as failure, 81, 131; as sign of authority, 116, 134; exploiting impotence, 97, 109–12, 126–7
incest, 86, 98, 101, 138n4
intersubjectivity, 12
Irwin, John, 138n5
Iser, Wolfgang, 40, 41, 109

Kenner, Hugh, 108

Lacan, Jacques, 8–10, 11–12, 99, 110–11, 117, 126–7, 137n6
Lawrence, D. H., 55

Man, Paul de 47–8
mimetic desire, 21, 34, 42, 57, 88–9
Milton, John, 54, 119

New Criticism, 1
Nietzsche, Friedrich, 4, 55, 115, 130, 139n9

Plato, 3, 90
Puritanism, 53, 64

reason: in Hegel, 5; in Freud, 6; as representation, 4–5, 80, 120, 127; as mastery, 129
repetition: of sin, 17, 23, 57, 91; and Freud, 8, 16, 78; Kierkegaardian, 48; and meaning, 16, 27, 120; and power, 23–4, 36–7; as revenge, 49, 81; as plagiarism, 119; and mirrors, 74–5; and fulfillment, 68, 124
Ricoeur, Paul, 15–6
Roustang, François, 136n1